MW00948126

Foreword

Ultimate Bread Machine Cookbook (2024 Edition) - A comprehensive guide through the art and science of bread-making with a machine, is a testament to the evolution of baking from ancient, manual tradition to modern, accessible craft.

Bread, in its myriad forms, has been the cornerstone of human nutrition and culture for thousands of years. It has symbolized sustenance, community, and tradition across civilizations. Today, the bread machine has revolutionized home baking, making the once labor-intensive process of bread-making an accessible and rewarding endeavor for enthusiasts and novices alike.

This book is a beacon for those embarking on their bread-making journey, offering a step-by-step guide that demystifies the process of creating the perfect loaf. The recipes within these pages cater to a wide range of preferences and dietary needs, from classic and multigrain to cheese, sweet, holiday, and even gluten-free bread. Each recipe is a doorway to exploring the rich diversity and potential of bread, made possible through the convenience of the bread machine.

This book doesn't just teach you how to follow recipes; it invites you to understand the why behind each step, the how behind each ingredient's interaction, and the infinite possibilities that lie in combining different flavors and textures.

For beginners, this book will be a patient teacher, guiding you through the initial uncertainties and leading you to a place of confidence and creativity in your baking. For the seasoned baker, it offers a treasure trove of ideas to expand your repertoire and challenge your skills. The "Ultimate Bread Machine Cookbook (2024 Edition)" is more than just a collection of recipes; it's a companion in your culinary journey, encouraging you to experiment, learn, and ultimately, revel in the joy of baking.

May this book inspire you to explore the vast world of bread, to share your creations with loved ones, and to discover the satisfaction that comes from baking the perfect loaf.

Happy Baking,

What is the Bread Machine?

The term "Bread Machine" typically refers to a home appliance designed for baking bread. It automates the process of bread-making, which includes mixing, kneading, rising, and baking. Here's a general overview of what a bread machine does and how it works:

- **Mixing and Kneading:** The machine mixes the ingredients that the user adds—usually water, flour, yeast, salt, and sometimes sugar and fats. The machine's paddle, located at the bottom of the bread pan, kneads the dough to develop the gluten.

- **Rising:** After kneading, the machine allows the dough to rise. This is done in a controlled, warm environment inside the machine to help the yeast ferment and the dough to increase in volume.

- **Baking:** Once the dough has risen, the machine then bakes the bread at a pre-set temperature. The entire process from start to finish can take several hours, depending on the specific recipe and machine settings.

- **Control Panel:** Bread machines come with various settings for different types of bread, such as white, whole wheat, French, and sweet bread. Some also have settings for making jams, cakes, and dough for pizzas or rolls that can be shaped and baked in a conventional oven.

- **Convenience and Customization:** The main advantages of a bread machine include the convenience of making bread at home with minimal manual effort and the ability to control the ingredients, which is great for those with dietary restrictions or preferences for certain types of flour or additives.

How does it work?

1. **Adding Ingredients:** The user measures and adds ingredients to the bread pan. The order in which ingredients are added can vary based on the machine's design or the specific recipe. Typically, liquids are added first, followed by the flour, and then the yeast is placed last to prevent it from contacting the liquid too early.

2. **Mixing:** Once the bread pan is placed inside the machine and the user selects the desired program, the machine starts the mixing phase. A small paddle, located at the bottom of the pan, moves in a circular motion to combine the ingredients into a dough.

3. **Kneading:** After mixing, the machine continues to knead the dough. This process is crucial for developing gluten, which gives the bread its structure and texture. Kneading is done by the paddle's continued motion, which stretches and folds the dough.

4. **First Rise:** The machine then allows the dough to rest and rise. This is a crucial step where the yeast ferments the sugars in the flour, producing carbon dioxide gas, which causes the dough to expand and rise. The machine maintains an optimal temperature to encourage this process.

5. **Punch Down and Second Rise (if applicable):** Some bread machine cycles include a "punch down" step, where the machine briefly kneads the dough again to expel any large gas bubbles. Then, the dough is allowed to rise a second time. This step may not be present in all cycles, depending on the type of bread being made.

6. **Baking:** After the rise phase(s), the machine heats up to bake the bread. The baking temperature and time are preset based on the selected program. During this phase, the dough transforms into a baked loaf, developing a crust and finishing the cooking process.

7. **Cooling:** Some machines switch to a warming or cooling mode after baking to allow the bread to cool down gently before removal. This helps prevent the bread from becoming soggy due to condensation.

8. **Completion:** Once the baking cycle is complete, the machine will typically signal the end of the program. The user can then remove the bread pan from the machine. The paddle often remains embedded in the bottom of the loaf and must be removed separately.

Tips and Tricks to using Bread Machine:

- **Read the Manual:** Different models have unique features and specifications. Familiarize yourself with your machine's capabilities, cycle options, and any pre-programmed settings.

- **Ingredient Temperature:** Use ingredients at room temperature unless the recipe specifies otherwise. Cold ingredients can affect yeast activity and the dough's rise.

- **Order of Ingredients:** Most bread machines recommend adding liquids first, then dry ingredients, with yeast last. This prevents the yeast from contacting liquid until the kneading begins, which is essential for proper activation.

- **Measuring Ingredients:** Precision matters. Use a kitchen scale for flour and other ingredients if possible, as cup measurements can be inconsistent. Always spoon flour into a measuring cup and level it off with a knife rather than scooping, which can compact the flour.

- **Check the Dough Consistency:** During the first few minutes of the kneading cycle, open the lid and check the dough. It should form a smooth, round ball. If it's too dry, add a teaspoon of water at a time. If too wet, add a tablespoon of flour at a time until the consistency is right.

- **Yeast Matters:** Use fresh yeast, and if using active dry instead of instant (bread machine yeast), it may need to be dissolved in water first (check your recipe and yeast packaging for guidance). Store yeast in a cool, dry place or in the refrigerator once opened.

- **Experiment with Ingredients:** After you're comfortable with basic recipes, start experimenting. Add nuts, dried fruits, or spices to the mix. However, add these at the beep or during the appropriate add-in cycle if your machine has one.

- **Bread Machine Mixes:** You can use pre-packaged bread mixes designed for bread machines. They can be a convenient and foolproof way to make bread, though making bread from scratch offers more flexibility and control over the ingredients.

- **Alternative Uses:** Besides bread, use your machine to make pizza dough, cakes, jams, and even meatloaf. The mix and bake settings are versatile tools for more than just bread.

- **Removing the Bread:** Once the bread is done, remove it from the pan by turning it upside down and gently shaking it. Let the bread cool on a wire rack to prevent it from becoming soggy.

- **Cleaning and Maintenance:** Always unplug the machine and let it cool down before cleaning. Never immerse the machine in water. Clean the baking pan and kneading paddle with warm, soapy water and a soft sponge. Wipe down the interior and exterior with a damp cloth.

- **Slicing Bread:** Use a bread knife or electric knife to slice homemade bread. It's easier to slice and results in more uniform slices if you let the bread cool completely.

Bread Machine Cycles

Bread machines come with a variety of cycles designed to make different types of bread and dough. Each cycle adjusts the kneading, rising, and baking times to match the specific needs of the bread type. Here's an overview of common bread machine cycles and what they're used for:

1. **Basic/White:** This cycle is for recipes that mostly contain white bread flour. It typically has a faster rise than whole wheat or other flours.
2. **Whole Wheat:** Designed for breads using a significant portion of whole wheat flour. This cycle includes longer rise times to accommodate the heavier flour.
3. **French/Italian:** For making light bread with a crispy crust and airy interior. These cycles often have longer kneading and rising times to develop the texture.
4. **Sweet:** Used for breads with higher amounts of sugar, fat, and protein (from eggs or milk), which can inhibit yeast growth. The cycle is adjusted to ensure proper rise despite these ingredients.
5. **Gluten-Free:** Specifically tailored for gluten-free bread recipes, taking into account the lack of gluten, which requires different kneading and rising patterns.
6. **Express/Fast Bake:** Offers a quicker bread-making process by reducing the time needed for rising. The texture of the bread might be slightly different from those using standard cycles.
7. **Dough:** This cycle prepares the dough for baking without actually baking it in the machine. It goes through the kneading and first rise, after which the dough is ready to be shaped, given a final rise, and then baked in a conventional oven. Great for pizza dough, rolls, and more.
8. **Jam:** Allows the machine to mix, heat, and cook ingredients to make jam or jelly.
9. **Fruit and Nut:** A program that will take the dry ingredients and mix them in with the wet ingredients and bake bread that is full of fruits, nuts, and grains.
10. **Vegetable:** A program that will bake bread with vegetables.
11. **Cake:** Mixes and bakes cake batter without the need for kneading. This cycle is for non-yeast breads that are chemically leavened (e.g., banana bread).
12. **Artisan Dough:** Provides a longer, cooler rise to develop flavors and textures similar to those in artisan bread, without actually baking the bread in the machine.
13. **Rye Bread:** Some machines have a specific setting for rye or other special flours, accounting for different kneading and rising needs.
14. **Pasta Dough:** For mixing and kneading dough that will be used to make pasta. No baking is involved in this cycle.

TABLE OF CONTENTS

TABLE OF CONTENTS

TABLE OF CONTENTS

GLUTEN-FREE BREAD

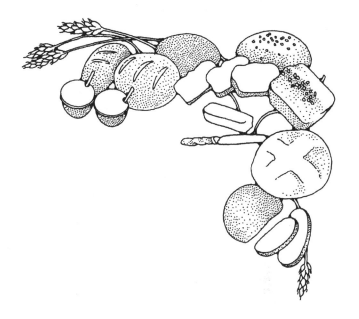

White Bread

Prep: 10 Min

Serves: 1 loaf (12 slices)

Ingredient:

- 1 cup + 2 tablespoons water (270 ml), 80°F (27°C)
- 1 teaspoon sugar (4.2 g)
- 1½ teaspoons salt (8.54 g)
- 3 cups bread flour (381 g)
- 1½ teaspoons active dry yeast (4.65 g)

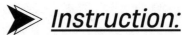 ## Instruction:

1. Preparation: Ensure that the water is at the correct temperature (27°C) to activate the yeast effectively.
2. Add Ingredients to Bread Maker: Add the ingredients to your bread machine in the order recommended by the manufacturer. Typically, this involves adding liquids first, followed by dry ingredients, with yeast added last to prevent it from coming into contact with the liquid too early.
3. Select Program: Set your bread machine to the Basic or White Bread setting. Choose a light crust color if your machine has this option.
4. Start the Bread Machine: Close the lid and press the start button to begin the bread-making process.
5. Baking Cycle: The bread machine will mix, knead, rise, and bake the bread automatically.
6. End of Baking: Once the baking cycle is complete, carefully remove the bread pan from the machine using oven mitts. Let the bread rest in the pan for about 5 minutes before removing it.
7. Cooling: Transfer the bread to a wire rack and allow it to cool completely before slicing. This ensures the best texture and ease of slicing.

CHAPTER 01: CLASSIC BREAD

Whole Wheat Bread

Prep: 10 Min

Serves: 1 loaf (12 slices)

Ingredient:

- 1¼ cups water (310 ml), 80°F (27°C)
- 2 tablespoons olive oil (30 ml)
- 3 tablespoons honey (63 g)
- 2 cups whole wheat flour (240 g)
- 1 cup bread flour (127 g)
- 1 teaspoon salt (5.69 g)
- 1½ teaspoons active dry yeast (4.65 g

Instruction:

1. Prepare the Ingredients: Ensure all ingredients are measured accurately and prepared as listed. The water should be at the specified temperature to optimize yeast activation.
2. Layer the Ingredients: In the bread pan, add the ingredients in the following order: water, olive oil, honey, whole wheat flour, bread flour, and salt. Make a small indentation on top of the flour (but not reaching the wet layer) and add the yeast into this indentation.
3. Select the Program: On your bread maker, select the Whole Wheat Program. This setting is optimized for the heavier texture of whole wheat flour. Choose your crust color preference if your machine offers this option.
4. Start the Bread Maker: Close the lid and press the start button. The machine will take care of kneading, rising, and baking the bread.
5. Cooling the Bread: Once the baking cycle is complete, the bread maker will signal its finish. Carefully remove the bread pan using oven mitts, turn it over, and gently shake the loaf out onto a cooling rack. Allow the bread to cool completely for about 1 hour. This step is crucial for texture and ease of slicing.
6. Serve: Slice the bread with a serrated knife to get even slices. Enjoy your homemade whole wheat bread as a healthy addition to your meals or a tasty snack on its own.

French Bread

Prep: 10 Min

Serves: 1 loaf (16 slices)

Ingredient:

- 1½ cups water (355 ml), 80°F (27°C)
- 1 tablespoon sugar (12.6 g)
- 1½ teaspoons salt (8.54 g)
- 4 cups all-purpose flour (480 g)
- 2¼ teaspoons active dry yeast (7 g)

 ## Instruction:

1. Add Ingredients to Bread Pan: Start by adding the water to the bread pan. Next, add the sugar and salt. Carefully add the flour, covering the liquid. Make a small indentation on top of the flour and add the yeast into this well. Ensure the yeast does not come into direct contact with the liquid.
2. Select Bread Maker Settings: For French Bread, select the French Program. This setting is tailored for recipes that require a longer rise time, which is typical for French Bread. If your machine allows you to choose the crust color, select your preference.
3. Start the Bread Maker: Close the lid of the bread maker and press the start button. The machine will mix, knead, rise, and bake the bread.
4. Cool the Bread: Once the bread maker completes its cycle and beeps, carefully remove the bread pan using oven mitts. Turn the pan upside down and gently shake to release the bread onto a wire rack. Allow the bread to cool for at least 1 hour before slicing. Cooling is essential for the structure and texture of the bread.
5. Slice and Enjoy: Use a serrated knife to slice the bread. French Bread is known for its crispy crust and soft interior, making it ideal for sandwiches, serving with cheese, or simply enjoying with butter.

CHAPTER 01: CLASSIC BREAD

Italian Bread

Prep: 10 Min

Serves: 1 loaf (12 slices)

Ingredient:

- 1 cup + 2 tablespoons water (270 ml), 80°F (27°C)
- 1½ tablespoons olive oil (22.5 ml)
- 1½ teaspoons sugar (6.3 g)
- 1½ teaspoons salt (8.54 g)
- 3 cups all-purpose flour (360 g)
- 1½ teaspoons active dry yeast (4.65 g)
- 1 teaspoon dried Italian herbs (optional for flavor) (2.8 g)

 ## Instruction:

1. Layer Ingredients in Bread Pan: Begin by adding the water and olive oil to the bread pan. Then, sprinkle the sugar and salt. Add the all-purpose flour, spreading it evenly over the liquid ingredients. If using, sprinkle the dried Italian herbs over the flour. Create a small indentation on top of the flour and carefully add the yeast to this indentation.
2. Select the Program: On your bread maker, select the French setting since Italian Bread typically requires a similar process. Adjust the crust color setting according to your preference.
3. Start the Bread Maker: Close the lid of the bread maker and press the start button. The machine will mix, knead, rise, and bake the bread through its cycle.
4. Cool the Bread: Once the cycle is complete and the machine signals the end, carefully remove the bread pan with oven mitts. Turn the pan over to gently release the bread onto a wire cooling rack. It's important to let the bread cool down for about 1 hour before slicing to allow the structure to set properly.
5. Serve: Slice the bread with a serrated knife for even pieces. Italian Bread, with its soft interior and crusty exterior, is perfect for dipping in olive oil, serving alongside pasta dishes, or making hearty sandwiches.

Multigrain Bread

Prep: 10 Min

Serves: 1 loaf (12 slices)

Ingredient:

- 1 cup + 2 tablespoons water (270 ml), 80°F (27°C)
- 2 tablespoons olive oil (30 ml)
- 1 teaspoon sugar (4.2 g)
- 1½ teaspoons salt (8.54 g)
- 2 cups bread flour (254 g)
- 1 cup multigrain flour (128 g) (If multigrain flour is not available, use a mix of whole wheat flour and a tablespoon each of flaxseeds, sunflower seeds, and oats to equal 1 cup)
- 1½ teaspoons active dry yeast (4.65 g)
- ¼ cup mixed seeds (sunflower, pumpkin, flaxseed) for inclusion in the dough (optional) (60 g)

➤ Instruction:

1. Add Ingredients to Bread Pan: Start by adding the water and olive oil to the bread maker pan. Follow with sugar and salt. Next, add the bread flour and multigrain flour. If you're using additional mixed seeds, sprinkle them over the flour. Lastly, make a small indentation on top of the flour (not deep enough to reach the liquid) and add the yeast into this well.
2. Select the Program: Use the Whole Wheat or Multigrain setting if your bread maker has one, as these settings are designed to accommodate the denser texture of multigrain bread. Choose your preferred crust color if this option is available.
3. Start the Bread Maker: Close the lid and start the bread maker. The machine will mix, knead, rise, and bake the bread.
4. Cooling the Bread: Once the bread maker finishes its cycle, carefully remove the bread pan using oven mitts. Invert the pan and gently shake to release the bread. Allow the bread to cool on a wire rack for at least 1 hour to improve its texture and make slicing easier.
5. Slice and Serve: With a serrated bread knife, slice the bread. Multigrain Bread is hearty and flavorful, perfect for sandwiches or toasted with butter.

CHAPTER 01: CLASSIC BREAD

Rye Bread

Prep: 10 Min

Serves: 1 loaf (12 slices)

Ingredient:

- 1 cup + 1 tablespoon water (255 ml), 80°F (27°C)
- 1½ tablespoons molasses (22.5 ml)
- 1 tablespoon olive oil (15 ml)
- 1½ teaspoons salt (8.54 g)
- 2 cups bread flour (254 g)
- 1 cup rye flour (102 g)
- 2 teaspoons caraway seeds (optional for flavor) (5.6 g)
- 1½ teaspoons active dry yeast (4.65 g)

➤ Instruction:

1. Layer Ingredients in Bread Pan: Begin by adding the water, molasses, and olive oil to the bread pan. Follow with adding the salt, bread flour, and rye flour. If using, sprinkle the caraway seeds over the flour. Finally, make a small indentation on top of the flour (without reaching the liquid) and add the yeast into this well.
2. Select the Program: Choose the Rye or Whole Wheat setting if your bread maker has it, as these settings typically provide a longer rise time suitable for rye bread dough. Select your preferred crust color if your machine offers this option.
3. Start the Bread Maker: Close the lid of the bread maker and start the program. The machine will take care of mixing, kneading, rising, and baking the bread.
4. Cool the Bread: Once the bread is done and the machine beeps, carefully remove the bread pan using oven mitts. Invert the pan and gently tap it to release the bread. Let the bread cool on a wire rack for about an hour before slicing, to ensure the texture settles properly.
5. Slice and Serve: Use a serrated knife to slice the bread. Rye Bread, with its distinctive flavor enhanced by molasses and optional caraway seeds, is excellent for sandwiches or as an accompaniment to soups and salads.

Pumpernickel Bread

Prep: 10 Min

Serves: 1 loaf (12 slices)

Ingredient:

- 1 cup + 2 tablespoons water (270 ml), 80°F (27°C)
- 2 tablespoons molasses (30 ml)
- 1½ tablespoons unsweetened cocoa powder (11.25 g)
- 1 tablespoon butter, softened (14 g)
- 1½ teaspoons salt (8.54 g)
- 1½ cups rye flour (180 g)
- 1½ cups bread flour (180 g)
- 2 teaspoons caraway seeds (optional for authentic flavor) (5.6 g)
- 1½ teaspoons active dry yeast (4.65 g)

 ## Instruction:

1. Add Ingredients to Bread Pan: Begin by adding the water, molasses, cocoa powder, and butter to the bread pan. Follow with the salt, rye flour, bread flour, and, if using, caraway seeds. Create a small indentation on top of the flour mixture without going through to the liquid, and add the yeast to this indentation.
2. Select the Program: If your bread maker has a Whole Wheat or Dark Bread setting, select it, as Pumpernickel is a denser and darker bread that benefits from longer rise times. Choose your crust color preference if available.
3. Start the Bread Maker: Close the lid and start the bread maker. The machine will mix, knead, rise, and bake the bread.
4. Cool the Bread: Once the baking cycle is complete, remove the bread pan from the machine using oven mitts. Turn the pan over to gently release the bread onto a wire rack. Allow the bread to cool for about 1 hour before slicing. This step is important for texture and ease of slicing.
5. Slice and Enjoy: With a serrated knife, slice the bread. Pumpernickel Bread is known for its rich, deep flavors, enhanced by molasses and cocoa powder, making it perfect for sandwiches or as an accompaniment to hearty soups and stews.

CHAPTER 01: CLASSIC BREAD

Sourdough Bread

Prep: 10 Min

Serves: 1 loaf (12 slices)

Ingredient:

- 1 cup sourdough starter (240 ml)
- ½ cup + 2 tablespoons water (150 ml), 80°F (27°C)
- 1½ teaspoons salt (8.54 g)
- 2 tablespoons sugar (25.2 g)
- 3 cups bread flour (381 g)
- 1½ teaspoons active dry yeast (4.65 g)

Instruction:

1. Prepare the Bread Maker: Place the sourdough starter and water into the bread machine pan. Ensure the water is at the appropriate temperature of 80°F (27°C) to not shock the starter.
2. Add the Dry Ingredients: Add the salt and sugar over the liquid. Then, carefully add the bread flour. Spread the flour evenly to cover the wet ingredients. Make a small indentation on top of the flour (but not deep enough to reach the wet mixture) and add the yeast to this indentation.
3. Select the Program: Use the Sourdough or Basic setting on your bread maker. (The Sourdough setting is designed for recipes that include a sourdough starter, but the Basic setting is an adequate alternative). Choose your crust color preference if your machine offers this option.
4. Start the Bread Maker: Close the lid and start the machine. It will mix, knead, and bake the bread.
5. Cool the Bread: Once the baking cycle is complete, remove the bread pan from the machine with oven mitts. Invert the pan to gently release the bread onto a wire rack. Let the bread cool for about 1 hour before slicing. Cooling helps to set the crumb and crust, making slicing easier.
6. Serve: Slice the bread with a serrated knife. Sourdough bread is renowned for its tangy flavor and chewy texture, making it excellent for sandwiches, toast, or to enjoy with soup.

Ciabatta

Prep: 10 Min

Serves: 1 loaf (12 slices)

Ingredient:

- 1 cup + 2 tablespoons water (270 ml), 80°F (27°C)
- 1½ teaspoons olive oil (7.5 ml)
- 1 teaspoon sugar (4.2 g)
- 1½ teaspoons salt (8.54 g)
- 3 cups bread flour (381 g)
- 1½ teaspoons active dry yeast (4.65 g)

 ## Instruction:

1. Add Ingredients to Bread Maker: Begin by adding the water and olive oil to the bread maker pan. Next, add the sugar and salt. Then, carefully add the bread flour. Finally, make a small indentation on top of the flour (but not deep enough to reach the wet ingredients) and add the yeast into this indentation.
2. Select Dough Setting: For Ciabatta, we need to use the dough setting on your bread maker because Ciabatta is typically shaped and then baked in a conventional oven to achieve its characteristic crust and airy texture. Start the bread maker.
3. Preheat Oven: While the dough is being prepared, preheat your oven to 425°F (220°C).
4. Shaping the Dough: Once the dough cycle is complete, gently remove the dough (it will be sticky) onto a well-floured surface. Shape it into a rectangle or two loaves without overworking the dough to keep the air bubbles intact.
5. Second Rise: Place the shaped dough onto a baking sheet lined with parchment paper. Cover loosely with a damp cloth and let it rise in a warm place for about 30 minutes, or until slightly puffed.
6. Bake: Transfer the baking sheet to the preheated oven and bake for 25 to 30 minutes, or until the bread is golden brown and sounds hollow when tapped on the bottom.
7. Cool: Remove the Ciabatta from the oven and let it cool on a wire rack for at least 20 minutes before slicing. This resting period helps develop the bread's internal structure.
8. Serve: Slice the Ciabatta and serve. It's excellent for sandwiches or as an accompaniment to meals, especially with olive oil for dipping.

CHAPTER 01: CLASSIC BREAD

Focaccia

Prep: 10 Min

Serves: 8-10

Ingredient:

- 1 cup + 2 tablespoons water (270 ml), 80°F (27°C)
- 2 tablespoons olive oil (30 ml), plus extra for topping
- 1½ teaspoons salt (8.54 g)
- 3 cups bread flour (381 g)
- 1 teaspoon sugar (4.2 g)
- 2 teaspoons active dry yeast (6.2 g)
- Optional toppings: rosemary, coarse salt, cherry tomatoes, olives, etc.

Instruction:

1. Add Ingredients to Bread Maker: Begin by adding the water, 2 tablespoons of olive oil, and then the salt to the bread maker pan. Next, add the bread flour. Sprinkle the sugar evenly over the flour. Finally, make a small indentation on top of the flour (but not deep enough to reach the wet ingredients) and add the yeast into this indentation.
2. Select Dough Setting: Choose the dough setting on your bread maker and start it. This will mix, knead, and rise the dough.
3. Preheat Oven: While the dough is in the bread maker, preheat your oven to 425°F (220°C).
4. Prepare the Dough: Once the dough cycle is complete, gently remove the dough and place it on a lightly floured surface. Stretch the dough to fit a lightly oiled baking sheet or round pizza pan.
5. Add Toppings: Drizzle the top of the dough with olive oil and gently press your fingertips into the dough to create dimples. Sprinkle your chosen toppings over the dough, such as rosemary, coarse salt, cherry tomatoes, or olives.
6. Second Rise: Let the dough rest and rise for about 20 minutes in a warm place, or until slightly puffed.
7. Bake: Place the baking sheet in the preheated oven and bake for 20-25 minutes, or until the focaccia is golden brown and delicious.
8. Cool and Serve: Remove the focaccia from the oven and let it cool slightly on a wire rack before cutting into pieces and serving.

Brioche

Prep: 10 Min

Serves: 1 loaf (16 slices)

Ingredient:

- ¾ cup milk (180 ml), 80°F (27°C)
- 3 large eggs (lightly beaten, total volume approximately 150 ml)
- 2 tablespoons sugar (25.2 g)
- 1½ teaspoons salt (8.54 g)
- 3½ cups bread flour (445 g)
- 1 cup unsalted butter (227 g), softened and cut into small pieces
- 2 teaspoons active dry yeast (6.2 g)

Instruction:

1. Add Liquid Ingredients: Start by adding the warm milk (80°F or 27°C) to the bread maker pan. Next, add the lightly beaten eggs.
2. Add Dry Ingredients: Sprinkle the sugar and salt over the liquids. Add the bread flour, ensuring it covers the wet ingredients. Place the softened butter pieces evenly on top of the flour.
3. Add Yeast: Make a small indentation in the center of the flour (but not deep enough to reach the liquid) and add the yeast into this well.
4. Select the Sweet Bread Cycle: Since Brioche is a type of sweet bread with a high fat and egg content, select the Sweet Bread Cycle on your bread maker. This cycle is optimized for doughs with higher fat and sugar contents.
5. Start the Bread Maker: Close the lid and start the bread maker. The machine will mix, knead, rise, and bake the Brioche.
6. Baking Completion: Once the baking cycle is complete, carefully remove the bread pan from the machine. Let the Brioche sit in the pan for about 5-10 minutes before turning it out onto a wire rack.
7. Cool and Serve: Allow the Brioche to cool completely on a wire rack before slicing. This ensures the texture sets properly for that classic tender crumb.

CHAPTER 01: CLASSIC BREAD

Baguette

Prep: 10 Min

Serves: 2 baguettes

Ingredient:

- 1 cup + 2 tablespoons water (270 ml), 80°F (27°C)
- 1½ teaspoons salt (8.54 g)
- 3 cups bread flour (381 g)
- 1½ teaspoons active dry yeast (4.65 g)

Instruction:

1. Add Ingredients to Bread Maker: Place the water into the bread maker pan. Next, add the salt, followed by the bread flour. Finally, make a small indentation in the flour and add the yeast to this indentation. Ensure the yeast does not touch the liquid directly.
2. Select the Dough Cycle: Choose the Dough cycle on your bread maker. This cycle will mix, knead, and undergo the first rise of the dough within the machine.
3. Preheat the Oven: When the dough cycle is nearly complete, preheat your oven to 475°F (245°C).
4. Shape the Dough: Once the dough cycle is finished, remove the dough from the bread maker. On a lightly floured surface, divide the dough into two equal parts. Roll each part into a long, thin shape, approximately 16 inches long. Place on a baguette pan or a baking sheet lined with parchment paper.
5. Second Rise: Cover the shaped dough with a clean kitchen towel and let it rise in a warm place for about 30 minutes, or until slightly puffed.
6. Prepare for Baking: Just before baking, make several diagonal slashes on the top of each baguette with a sharp knife. Optionally, mist the baguettes lightly with water to help create a crispy crust.
7. Bake: Place the baguettes in the preheated oven. For an extra crispy crust, you can place a pan of water on the bottom rack of the oven to create steam. Bake for about 25 minutes, or until the baguettes are golden brown and sound hollow when tapped on the bottom.
8. Cool and Serve: Remove the baguettes from the oven and cool on a wire rack before slicing.

Challah

Prep: 10 Min

Serves: 1 loaf (12 slices)

Ingredient:

- ¾ cup water (180 ml), 80°F (27°C)
- 2 large eggs (lightly beaten, total volume approximately 100 ml)
- 4 tablespoons oil (60 ml)
- 4 tablespoons honey (85 g)
- 1½ teaspoons salt (8.54 g)
- 3 cups bread flour (381 g)
- 1½ teaspoons active dry yeast (4.65 g)

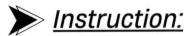

Instruction:

1. Add Ingredients to Bread Maker: Start by adding the water, beaten eggs, oil, and honey to the bread maker pan. Then, add the salt and bread flour. Make a small indentation on top of the flour (but not deep enough to reach the wet ingredients) and add the yeast to this indentation.
2. Select the Dough Cycle: Since Challah requires braiding and baking in a conventional oven to achieve its characteristic appearance and texture, use the Dough cycle on your bread maker. This cycle will mix, knead, and rise the dough.
3. Preheat the Oven: Once the Dough cycle is complete, preheat your oven to 375°F (190°C).
4. Braid the Dough: Remove the dough from the bread maker and divide it into the desired number of strands for braiding (commonly three or six). Braid the strands and place the braided loaf on a baking sheet lined with parchment paper.
5. Second Rise: Cover the braided dough loosely with a clean kitchen towel and let it rise in a warm place until it's puffy, about 30 to 45 minutes.
6. Egg Wash (optional): For a shiny crust, you can brush the loaf with an egg wash (1 beaten egg mixed with 1 tablespoon of water) before baking.
7. Bake: Bake in the preheated oven for 25 to 30 minutes, or until the Challah is golden brown and sounds hollow when tapped on the bottom.
8. Cool and Serve: Remove the Challah from the oven and let it cool on a wire rack before slicing.

CHAPTER 01: CLASSIC BREAD

Potato Bread

Prep: 15 Min

Serves: 1 loaf (12 slices)

Ingredient:

- 1 cup water (240 ml), 80°F (27°C)
- ½ cup mashed potatoes (120 ml or approximately 115 g, cooled to room temperature)
- 2 tablespoons butter (28.4 g), softened
- 1½ teaspoons salt (8.54 g)
- 2 tablespoons sugar (25.2 g)
- 3 cups bread flour (381 g)
- 2 teaspoons active dry yeast (6.2 g)

Instruction:

1. Prepare Mashed Potatoes: If you haven't already, boil or steam potatoes until tender, then mash until smooth. Allow the mashed potatoes to cool to room temperature before using.
2. Add Ingredients to Bread Maker: Start by adding the water and mashed potatoes to the bread maker pan. Add the butter in small pieces. Next, sprinkle in the salt and sugar. Add the bread flour, covering the wet ingredients. Make a small indentation on top of the flour (but not deep enough to reach the wet ingredients) and add the yeast to this well.
3. Select the Basic Cycle: Choose the Basic or White Bread setting on your bread maker. If your machine offers crust color settings, select your preference.
4. Start the Bread Maker: Close the lid and start the bread maker. The machine will mix, knead, rise, and bake the Potato Bread.
5. Wait for Completion: Once the bread maker completes its cycle, carefully remove the bread pan from the machine using oven mitts. Let the bread sit in the pan for about 5-10 minutes before turning it out onto a wire rack.
6. Cool and Serve: Allow the Potato Bread to cool completely on a wire rack before slicing to ensure the best texture and flavor.

Gluten-Free Bread

Prep: 10 Min

Serves: 1 loaf (12 slices)

Ingredient:

- 1½ cups warm water (360 ml), 80°F (27°C)
- 3 tablespoons olive oil (45 ml)
- 2 teaspoons cider vinegar (10 ml)
- 3 cups gluten-free flour blend (360 g)
- 1 teaspoon salt (5.69 g)
- 2 tablespoons sugar (25.2 g)
- 2½ teaspoons (one packet) active dry yeast (7.5 g)
- 1½ teaspoons xanthan gum (if not included in your flour blend) (4.65 g)

 ## Instruction:

1. Add Wet Ingredients: Pour the warm water, olive oil, and cider vinegar into the bread maker pan.
2. Add Dry Ingredients: Next, add the gluten-free flour blend. On top of the flour, evenly distribute the salt and sugar. If your gluten-free flour blend does not include xanthan gum, sprinkle it over the flour as well.
3. Add Yeast: Make a small well in the center of the dry ingredients (not reaching down to the wet) and add the yeast.
4. Select the Gluten-Free Cycle: Choose the Gluten-Free Cycle on your bread maker. This cycle is specifically designed for gluten-free bread recipes, accommodating the unique mixing, rising, and baking needs of gluten-free dough.
5. Start the Bread Maker: Close the lid and start the cycle. The bread maker will mix, knead, rise, and bake the bread.
6. Cool Before Slicing: Once the cycle is complete, carefully remove the bread pan from the machine. Let the bread cool in the pan for 10-15 minutes before transferring it to a wire rack to cool completely. Gluten-free bread can be more fragile when hot, so this step helps it maintain its structure.
7. Serve: Once cooled, slice the bread. Gluten-free bread is best enjoyed the day it's made but can be stored in an airtight container or frozen for later use.

CHAPTER 01: CLASSIC BREAD

Cornbread

Prep: 10 Min

Serves: 1 loaf or cake (serves 8–10)

Ingredient:

- 1 cup milk (240 ml), 80°F (27°C)
- ¼ cup unsalted butter (60 g), melted
- 2 large eggs
- 1 cup cornmeal (120 g)
- 1 cup all-purpose flour (120 g)
- ¼ cup sugar (50 g)
- 1 tablespoon baking powder (14 g)
- ½ teaspoon salt (2.9 g)

 ## Instruction:

1. Prepare Ingredients: Lightly beat the eggs. Ensure the milk is warmed to 80°F (27°C) and the butter is melted.
2. Add Ingredients to Bread Maker: If your bread maker instructions suggest adding liquids first, start with the milk, melted butter, and eggs. Then, add the cornmeal, all-purpose flour, sugar, baking powder, and salt. If your bread maker has a different recommendation for adding ingredients, follow that guidance.
3. Select the Cake Cycle: Choose the Cake or Quick Bread cycle on your bread maker. This cycle is designed for batters rather than traditional yeast bread dough.
4. Start the Bread Maker: Close the lid and start the cycle. The machine will mix the ingredients and bake the cornbread.
5. Monitoring: Some bread makers may require manual intervention to scrape down the sides of the pan with a silicone spatula during the mixing phase. If your machine has a viewing window, you can check to see if this is necessary.
6. Cool Before Serving: Once the cycle is complete, carefully remove the bread pan from the machine and allow the cornbread to cool for a few minutes before transferring it to a wire rack to cool further.
7. Serve: Cornbread can be served warm or at room temperature. It pairs wonderfully with chili, soups, or as a standalone snack

Milk Bread (Shokupan)

Prep: 10   Min

Serves: 1 loaf (12 slices)

Ingredient:

- 1 cup + 1 tablespoon milk (255 ml), 80°F (27°C)
- 2 tablespoons sugar (25.2 g)
- 2 tablespoons unsalted butter (28.4 g), softened
- 1½ teaspoons salt (8.54 g)
- 3 cups bread flour (381 g)
- 2 teaspoons active dry yeast (6.2 g)

 ## Instruction:

1. Prepare the Ingredients: Ensure the milk is warmed to 80°F (27°C) to activate the yeast effectively. The butter should be softened to room temperature.
2. Add Ingredients to Bread Maker: Begin by adding the milk to the bread maker pan. Follow with the sugar, softened butter, and salt. Next, add the bread flour. Make a small indentation on top of the flour (but not deep enough to reach the wet ingredients) and add the yeast to this well.
3. Select the Basic or White Bread Cycle: Choose the Basic or White Bread setting on your bread maker. This cycle is suitable for milk bread due to its kneading, rising, and baking requirements. If your machine offers crust color settings, select your preference.
4. Start the Bread Maker: Close the lid and start the cycle. The machine will mix, knead, rise, and bake the Milk Bread.
5. Wait for Completion: Once the baking cycle is complete, carefully remove the bread pan from the machine using oven mitts. Let the Milk Bread sit in the pan for about 5-10 minutes before turning it out onto a wire rack.
6. Cool and Serve: Allow the Milk Bread to cool completely on a wire rack before slicing. This bread is known for its soft texture and is ideal for sandwiches or simply enjoying with butter or jam.

CHAPTER 01: CLASSIC BREAD

Spelt Bread

Prep: 10   Min

Serves: 1 loaf (12 slices)

Ingredient:

- 1¼ cups water (300 ml), 80°F (27°C)
- 2 tablespoons olive oil (30 ml)
- 2 tablespoons honey (42 g)
- 1½ teaspoons salt (8.54 g)
- 3 cups spelt flour (360 g) - If using whole spelt flour, the measurements remain the same.
- 2 teaspoons active dry yeast (6.2 g)

 ## Instruction:

1. Add Liquid Ingredients: Begin by adding the water, olive oil, and honey to the bread maker pan. These liquid ingredients should be at 80°F (27°C) to ensure the yeast activates properly.
2. Add Dry Ingredients: Add the salt and then the spelt flour on top of the liquid ingredients. It's important to cover the liquids completely with the flour to prevent the yeast from activating too early.
3. Add Yeast: Make a small well in the center of the flour (but not deep enough to reach the liquid) and add the yeast to this indentation. This placement helps ensure the yeast is activated at the right time during the kneading process.
4. Select the Whole Wheat Cycle: Choose the Whole Wheat setting on your bread maker.
5. Start the Bread Maker: Close the lid and start the cycle. The machine will mix, knead, rise, and bake the Spelt Bread.
6. Cool Before Slicing: Once the cycle is complete, carefully remove the bread pan from the machine. Let the Spelt Bread sit in the pan for about 5-10 minutes before turning it out onto a wire rack to cool completely. This cooling time helps improve the bread's texture and makes it easier to slice.
7. Serve: Slice the bread using a serrated knife to get even slices. Spelt Bread is delicious when served fresh and pairs well with a variety of spreads and toppings.

Oat Bread

Prep: 10 Min

Serves: 1 loaf (12 slices)

Ingredient:

- 1 cup + 2 tablespoons water (270 ml), 80°F (27°C)
- 2 tablespoons unsalted butter (28.4 g), softened
- 2 tablespoons honey (42 g)
- 1½ teaspoons salt (8.54 g)
- 2 cups bread flour (254 g)
- 1 cup rolled oats (90 g), plus extra for topping
- 2 teaspoons active dry yeast (6.2 g)

 Instruction:

1. Add Wet Ingredients to Bread Maker: Begin by adding the water, softened butter, and honey to the bread maker pan.
2. Add Dry Ingredients: Add the salt, then the bread flour. Add the rolled oats on top of the flour. Make a small indentation in the center of the dry ingredients (but not deep enough to reach the wet) and add the yeast to this well.
3. Select the Basic or Whole Wheat Cycle: Choose the Basic Cycle for a softer loaf or the Whole Wheat Cycle if your machine has it, for a denser texture.
4. Start the Bread Maker: Close the lid and start the selected cycle. The bread maker will mix, knead, rise, and bake the bread.
5. Optional: Oat Topping: If your bread maker has a nut/fruit beep, you can add some extra rolled oats at this signal for a textured topping. If not, you can simply sprinkle some oats on top of the loaf before the final rise phase.
6. Cool Before Slicing: Once the cycle is complete, carefully remove the bread pan from the machine. Let the bread sit in the pan for about 10 minutes, then turn it out onto a wire rack to cool completely.
7. Serve: Slice the oat bread and enjoy. It's excellent for toast, sandwiches, or as a side with your meals.

CHAPTER 01: CLASSIC BREAD

Artisan Bread

Prep: 10 Min

Serves: 1 large loaf or 2 smaller loaves

Ingredient:

- 1½ cups water (360 ml), 80°F (27°C)
- 1 teaspoon salt (5.69 g)
- 1 tablespoon sugar (12.6 g)
- 4 cups all-purpose or bread flour (508 g)
- 1½ teaspoons active dry yeast (4.65 g)

Instruction:

1. Prepare the Dough: Add the water to the bread maker pan. Next, add the salt, sugar, and flour. Make a small indentation in the flour and add the yeast. Select the Dough cycle on your bread maker and start the machine. The bread maker will mix, knead, and let the dough rise once.
2. Shape the Dough: Once the Dough cycle is complete, gently remove the dough from the bread maker. On a lightly floured surface, shape the dough into a round loaf or two smaller loaves, depending on your preference. Avoid overworking the dough to maintain its airy structure.
3. Second Rise: Place the shaped dough on a parchment-lined baking sheet or a baker's peel if you're using a baking stone. Cover lightly with a clean kitchen towel and let it rise in a warm place until nearly doubled in size, about 30 to 45 minutes.
4. Preheat the Oven: While the dough is rising, preheat your oven to 450°F (232°C). If you have a baking stone, place it in the oven to preheat as well. If not, an inverted baking sheet or a Dutch oven can work.
5. Bake the Bread: Right before baking, make several slashes on the top of the dough with a sharp knife or lame. This allows the bread to expand freely. If you're using a baking stone, slide the dough onto the stone. If using a Dutch oven, place the dough inside and cover. Bake for about 25-30 minutes, or until the bread is golden brown and sounds hollow when tapped. If using a Dutch oven, remove the lid halfway through baking to develop a crust.
6. Cool Before Slicing: Let the bread cool on a wire rack for at least an hour before slicing. This resting period is crucial for developing the bread's texture and flavor.

Seven-Grain Bread

Prep: 10 Min

Serves: 1 loaf (12-16 slices)

Ingredient:

- 1¼ cups water (300 ml), 80°F (27°C)
- 2 tablespoons honey (42 g)
- 2 tablespoons olive oil (30 ml)
- 1½ teaspoons salt (8.54 g)
- 2 cups bread flour (254 g)
- 1 cup seven-grain cereal mix (dry) (160 g)
- 1½ teaspoons active dry yeast (4.65 g)

Instruction:

1. Add Liquid Ingredients to Bread Maker: Pour the water into the bread maker pan. Add the honey and olive oil next, ensuring they're evenly distributed.
2. Add Dry Ingredients: Sprinkle the salt into the pan. Add the bread flour, ensuring it covers the liquid ingredients. Then, evenly distribute the seven-grain cereal mix on top of the flour.
3. Add Yeast: Make a small well in the center of the dry ingredients (but not deep enough to reach the wet) and carefully add the yeast to this well.
4. Select the Appropriate Cycle: Choose the Whole Wheat or Multigrain Cycle on your bread maker. This cycle is designed to accommodate the heavier texture of multigrain bread and ensures proper mixing, kneading, rising, and baking.
5. Start the Bread Maker: Close the lid and start the selected cycle. The bread maker will do the rest, mixing the ingredients, kneading the dough, allowing it to rise, and baking the bread.
6. Wait and Remove: Once the baking cycle is complete, carefully remove the bread pan from the machine using oven mitts. Let the bread sit in the pan for about 5-10 minutes before turning it out onto a wire rack to cool.
7. Cool and Serve: Allow the Seven-Grain Bread to cool completely on a wire rack before slicing to ensure the best texture and flavor.

CHAPTER 02: MULTIGRAIN BREAD

Nine-Grain Bread

Prep: 10 Min

Serves: 1 loaf (12 slices)

Ingredient:

- 1 cup + 2 tablespoons water (270 ml), 80°F (27°C)
- 2 tablespoons olive oil (30 ml)
- 2 tablespoons honey (42 g)
- 1½ teaspoons salt (8.54 g)
- 3 cups bread flour (381 g)
- ½ cup nine-grain mix (use a pre-mixed nine-grain blend available at health food stores or make your own blend of grains such as wheat, barley, millet, rye, oats, amaranth, buckwheat, corn, and flaxseeds) (60 g)
- 1½ teaspoons active dry yeast (4.65 g)

Instruction:

1. Add Wet Ingredients: Pour the water into the bread maker pan. Add the olive oil and honey.
2. Add Dry Ingredients: Add the salt and then the bread flour. Sprinkle the nine-grain mix evenly over the flour. Make a small indentation on top of the dry ingredients (but not deep enough to reach the wet) and add the yeast to this well.
3. Select the Whole Wheat or Multigrain Cycle: Choose the cycle that best suits heavier bread with whole grains on your bread maker. This usually includes longer kneading and rising times to accommodate the whole grains.
4. Start the Bread Maker: Close the lid and start the selected cycle. The bread maker will mix, knead, rise, and bake the Nine-Grain Bread.
5. Cool Before Slicing: Once the cycle is complete, carefully remove the bread pan from the machine. Let the bread sit in the pan for about 10 minutes before turning it out onto a wire rack to cool completely.
6. Serve: Slice the cooled bread. Nine-Grain Bread is perfect for sandwiches or toasted with butter and jam.

Whole Wheat Multigrain Bread

Prep: 10 Min

Serves: 1 loaf (12 slices)

Ingredient:

- 1 cup + 2 tablespoons water (270 ml), 80°F (27°C)
- 2 tablespoons olive oil (30 ml)
- 2 tablespoons honey (42 g)
- 1½ teaspoons salt (8.54 g)
- 2 cups whole wheat flour (240 g)
- 1 cup multigrain flour blend (120 g) or a mix of additional grains like barley, oats, rye, and flaxseed
- ¼ cup sunflower seeds or mixed seeds (for example, a blend of sunflower, sesame, and flax seeds) (30 g)
- 1½ teaspoons active dry yeast (4.65 g)

Instruction:

1. Prepare the Bread Maker: Pour the water into the bread maker pan. Add the olive oil and honey.
2. Add Dry Ingredients: Sprinkle the salt over the liquid. Then, add the whole wheat flour and your choice of multigrain flour or additional grains. Add the sunflower seeds or mixed seeds over the flours. Make a small indentation on top of the dry ingredients (without reaching the wet) and add the yeast to this well.
3. Select the Cycle: Choose the Whole Wheat or Multigrain Cycle on your bread maker. This cycle is specially designed to handle the heavier dough consistency and longer rise times needed for whole wheat and multigrain bread.
4. Start the Bread Maker: Close the lid and start the cycle. The bread maker will mix, knead, rise, and bake the Whole Wheat Multigrain Bread.
5. Cooling: Once the baking cycle is complete, carefully remove the bread pan from the machine. Let the bread sit in the pan for about 10 minutes before removing it to cool completely on a wire rack. This helps the bread's structure to set and makes slicing easier.
6. Serve: Slice the bread once it has fully cooled. Whole Wheat Multigrain Bread is hearty and filling, perfect for sandwiches or toasted with your favorite spreads.

CHAPTER 02: MULTIGRAIN BREAD

Multigrain Sourdough Bread

Prep: At least 12 hours for sourdough starter preparation, plus 20 minutes for assembling and starting the dough

Serves: 1 loaf (12 slices)

Ingredient:

- 1 cup sourdough starter (240 ml), active and bubbly
- ¾ cup water (180 ml), room temperature
- 1 tablespoon honey (21 g)
- 1½ teaspoons salt (8.54 g)
- 2 cups bread flour (254 g)
- 1 cup multigrain flour (120 g) or a mix of whole wheat flour, rye flour, and additional grains such as barley, oats, and flaxseed
- 2 tablespoons mixed seeds (such as sunflower, sesame, or pumpkin seeds) (18 g)
- (Optional) Additional water or flour as needed to adjust dough consistency

Instruction:

1. Prepare the Sourdough Starter: Ensure your sourdough starter is active and bubbly by feeding it 12-24 hours before you plan to make the bread.
2. Mixing the Dough: Add the sourdough starter, water, and honey to the bread maker pan. Then add the salt, bread flour, and multigrain flour. Start the bread maker on the Dough cycle to mix and knead.
3. First Rise: If your bread maker has a Sourdough or Artisan cycle that allows for longer fermentation times, you can let the dough rise in the machine. Otherwise, after the dough is kneaded, transfer it to a large bowl, cover with a damp cloth, and let it rise at room temperature for 7-12 hours, or until roughly doubled in size.
4. Shape the Dough: Once the dough has risen, gently shape it into a loaf without deflating it too much.
5. Second Rise: Allow the shaped loaf to rise for another 1-2 hours, or until puffy and risen.
6. Preheat the Oven: Preheat your oven to 450°F (232°C) with a baking stone or Dutch oven inside.
7. Bake: Transfer the loaf onto a parchment paper to slide onto the baking stone or place inside the preheated Dutch oven. If using a baking stone, you might want to create steam by adding a pan of water to the oven. Bake for 30-40 minutes, or until the bread is golden brown and sounds hollow when tapped.
8. Cool: Let the bread cool on a wire rack for at least an hour before slicing.

Oat and Honey Multigrain Bread

Prep: 10 Min
Serves: 1 loaf (12 slices)

Ingredient:

- 1 cup + 2 tablespoons water (270 ml), 80°F (27°C)
- ¼ cup honey (85 g)
- 2 tablespoons olive oil (30 ml)
- 1½ teaspoons salt (8.54 g)
- 2 cups bread flour (254 g)
- 1 cup multigrain flour (120 g) or a combination of whole wheat flour, oats, and other grains like barley and rye
- ½ cup rolled oats (45 g), plus extra for topping
- 2 teaspoons active dry yeast (6.2 g)

 ## Instruction:

1. Add Liquids to Bread Maker Pan: Begin by pouring the water into the bread maker pan. Add the honey and olive oil.
2. Add Dry Ingredients: Sprinkle the salt over the liquids. Add the bread flour and multigrain flour or your combination of grains. Add the rolled oats. Make a small well in the center of the dry ingredients (without reaching the liquid) and add the yeast to this well.
3. Select the Cycle: Choose the Whole Wheat or Multigrain Cycle on your bread maker to accommodate the heavier dough consistency and longer rise times needed for multigrain bread.
4. Start the Bread Maker: Close the lid and start the selected cycle. The bread maker will mix, knead, rise, and bake the Bread.
5. If your bread maker has a nut/fruit beep, you can add some extra rolled oats at this signal for a textured topping. If not, you might be able to pause the machine just before the bake phase to sprinkle oats on top manually, depending on your model's features.
6. Once the cycle is complete, carefully remove the bread pan from the machine. Let the bread sit in the pan for about 10 minutes before removing it to cool completely on a wire rack.
7. Serve: Slice the bread once it has fully cooled. This Oat and Honey Multigrain Bread is perfect for breakfast toast, sandwiches, or simply enjoyed with a spread of butter.

Seeded Multigrain Bread

Prep: 10 Min
Serves: 1 loaf (12 slices)

Ingredient:

- 1 cup + 2 tablespoons water (270 ml), 80°F (27°C)
- 2 tablespoons olive oil (30 ml)
- 2 tablespoons honey (42 g)
- 1½ teaspoons salt (8.54 g)
- 2 cups bread flour (254 g)
- 1 cup multigrain flour (120 g), or a mix of whole wheat flour and your choice of additional grains (like barley, oats, and rye)
- ¼ cup sunflower seeds (35 g), plus extra for topping
- 2 tablespoons sesame seeds (18 g), plus extra for topping
- 2 tablespoons ground flax seeds (14 g)
- 2 teaspoons active dry yeast (6.2 g)

 ## Instruction:

1. Add Liquids to Bread Maker Pan: Pour the water into the bread maker pan. Add the olive oil and honey.
2. Add Dry Ingredients: Sprinkle the salt over the liquids. Add the bread flour and multigrain flour. Then, add the sunflower seeds, sesame seeds, and ground flax seeds. Make a small well in the center of the dry ingredients (without reaching the liquid) and add the yeast to this well.
3. Choose the Whole Wheat or Multigrain Cycle on your bread maker.
4. Close the lid and start the selected cycle. The bread maker will mix, knead, rise, and bake the Seeded Multigrain Bread.
5. Optional Seed Topping: If your bread maker has a nut/fruit beep, add some extra sunflower and sesame seeds at this signal for a textured topping. If not, you might be able to pause the machine just before the bake phase to add seeds on top manually, depending on your model's features.
6. Cool Before Slicing: Once the cycle is complete, carefully remove the bread pan from the machine. Let the bread sit in the pan for about 10 minutes before turning it out onto a wire rack to cool completely.
7. Serve: Slice the bread once it has fully cooled.

Rye Multigrain Bread

Prep: 10 Min

Serves: 1 loaf (12 slices)

Ingredient:

- 1 cup + 2 tablespoons water (270 ml), 80°F (27°C)
- 2 tablespoons olive oil (30 ml)
- 2 tablespoons molasses (42 g) for color and subtle sweetness
- 1½ teaspoons salt (8.54 g)
- 1 cup rye flour (102 g)
- 2 cups bread flour (254 g)
- ½ cup multigrain mix (a combination of whole wheat flour, oats, and other grains like barley) (60 g)
- ¼ cup sunflower seeds (35 g)
- 2 tablespoons sesame seeds (18 g)
- 2 tablespoons flax seeds (14 g)
- 2 teaspoons active dry yeast (6.2 g)

Instruction:

1. Prepare the Bread Maker: Pour the water into the bread maker pan. Add the olive oil and molasses.
2. Add Dry Ingredients: Sprinkle the salt over the liquid. Then, add the rye flour, bread flour, and your multigrain mix. On top of the flours, evenly distribute the sunflower seeds, sesame seeds, and flax seeds.
3. Add the Yeast: Make a small well in the center of the dry ingredients (but not deep enough to reach the liquid) and add the yeast to this well.
4. Select the Cycle: Choose the Whole Wheat or Multigrain Cycle on your bread maker. This cycle is designed for breads with heavier flours and additional grains and seeds, accommodating the longer kneading and rising times needed.
5. Close the lid and start the selected cycle. The bread maker will mix, knead, rise, and bake the Rye Multigrain Bread.
6. Cool Before Slicing: Once the cycle is complete, carefully remove the bread pan from the machine. Let the bread sit in the pan for about 10 minutes before turning it out onto a wire rack to cool completely.
7. Serve: Slice the bread once it has fully cooled. Rye Multigrain Bread is excellent for sandwiches or simply enjoyed with a spread of butter or cheese.

CHAPTER 02: MULTIGRAIN BREAD

Spelt Multigrain Bread

Prep: 10 Min

Serves: 1 loaf (12 slices)

Ingredient:

- 1 cup + 2 tablespoons water (270 ml), 80°F (27°C)
- 1 tablespoon olive oil (15 ml)
- 1 tablespoon honey (21 g)
- 1½ teaspoons salt (8.54 g)
- 2 cups spelt flour (240 g)
- 1 cup multigrain mix (this can include a combination of rolled oats, cracked wheat, barley, flaxseed, and sunflower seeds) (120 g)
- 2 teaspoons active dry yeast (6.2 g)

Instruction:

1. Add Liquids to Bread Maker Pan: Begin by pouring the water into the bread maker pan. Add the olive oil and honey.
2. Add Dry Ingredients: Next, add the salt. Then, layer in the spelt flour and your choice of multigrain mix. Ensure the grains and seeds are evenly distributed throughout the flour. Make a small indentation on top of the flour mix (but not deep enough to reach the wet ingredients) and add the yeast to this well.
3. Select the Appropriate Cycle: Choose the Whole Wheat or Multigrain Cycle on your bread maker to accommodate the heavier, denser nature of spelt and multigrain flours.
4. Start the Bread Maker: Close the lid and start the selected cycle. The bread maker will mix, knead, rise, and bake the Spelt Multigrain Bread.
5. Cool Before Slicing: Once the baking cycle is complete, carefully remove the bread pan from the machine. Let the bread sit in the pan for about 10 minutes before removing it to cool completely on a wire rack.
6. Serve: Slice the bread once it has fully cooled. Spelt Multigrain Bread is perfect for sandwiches, toasting, or enjoying with a generous spread of butter or jam.

Buckwheat Multigrain Bread

Prep: 10 Min

Serves: 1 loaf (12 slices)

Ingredient:

- 1 cup + 2 tablespoons water (270 ml), 80°F (27°C)
- 2 tablespoons olive oil (30 ml)
- 3 tablespoons honey (63 g)
- 1½ teaspoons salt (8.54 g)
- 1 cup buckwheat flour (120 g)
- 2 cups bread flour (254 g)
- ½ cup multigrain mix (such as rolled oats, flaxseeds, sunflower seeds, and sesame seeds) (60 g)
- 2 teaspoons active dry yeast (6.2 g)

Instruction:

1. Add Liquids to Bread Maker Pan: Pour the water into the bread maker pan. Add the olive oil and honey.
2. Add Dry Ingredients: Next, add the salt, buckwheat flour, and bread flour. Ensure the flours are evenly layered. Then, add your multigrain mix on top of the flours. Create a small well in the center of the flour (without reaching the liquid) and add the yeast to this well.
3. Select the Appropriate Cycle: Opt for the Whole Wheat or Multigrain Cycle on your bread maker. This setting is best suited for handling the heavier dough that comes with whole grains and seeds.
4. Start the Bread Maker: Close the lid and start the cycle. The machine will mix, knead, rise, and bake the Buckwheat Multigrain Bread.
5. Cool Before Slicing: Once the cycle is complete, carefully remove the bread pan from the machine. Let the bread sit in the pan for about 10 minutes before turning it out onto a wire rack to cool completely.
6. Serve: Slice the bread once it has fully cooled. Buckwheat Multigrain Bread is perfect for a hearty breakfast toast, delicious sandwiches, or as a complement to your favorite soups and stews.

CHAPTER 02: MULTIGRAIN BREAD

Barley Multigrain Bread

Prep: 10 Min

Serves: 1 loaf (12 slices)

Ingredient:

- 1 cup + 2 tablespoons water (270 ml), 80°F (27°C)
- 2 tablespoons olive oil (30 ml)
- 1 teaspoon sugar (4.2 g)
- 1½ teaspoons salt (8.54 g)
- 2 cups bread flour (254 g)
- 1 cup barley flour (120 g)
- ½ cup mixed grains (such as oats, flaxseed, and sunflower seeds) (60 g)
- 1½ teaspoons active dry yeast (4.65 g)

Instruction:

1. Add Liquids to Bread Maker Pan: Pour the water into the bread maker pan. Add the olive oil.
2. Add Dry Ingredients: Sprinkle the sugar and salt over the liquids. Then, add the bread flour and barley flour. Scatter the mixed grains over the flour. Make a small indentation in the center of the dry ingredients (but not deep enough to reach the wet) and add the yeast to this well.
3. Select the Appropriate Cycle: Choose the Whole Wheat or Multigrain Cycle on your bread maker to accommodate the heavier dough consistency and longer rise times needed for multigrain bread.
4. Start the Bread Maker: Close the lid and start the selected cycle. The bread maker will mix, knead, rise, and bake the Barley Multigrain Bread.
5. Cool Before Slicing: Once the cycle is complete, carefully remove the bread pan from the machine. Let the bread sit in the pan for about 10 minutes before turning it out onto a wire rack to cool completely.
6. Serve: Slice the bread once it has fully cooled. Barley Multigrain Bread is excellent for sandwiches, toasting, or simply enjoying with a spread of your favorite butter or jam.

Quinoa Multigrain Bread

Prep: 10   Min

Serves: 1 loaf (12 slices)

Ingredient:

- 1 cup + 2 tablespoons water (270 ml), 80°F (27°C)
- ¼ cup milk (60 ml), 80°F (27°C)
- 2 tablespoons olive oil (30 ml)
- 2 tablespoons honey (42 g)
- 1½ teaspoons salt (8.54 g)
- 2 cups bread flour (254 g)
- 1 cup whole wheat flour (120 g)
- ½ cup cooked quinoa (85 g), cooled
- ¼ cup mixed seeds (sunflower seeds, flaxseeds, sesame seeds) (30 g)
- 1½ teaspoons active dry yeast (4.65 g)

Instruction:

1. Prepare the Ingredients: Ensure the quinoa is cooked according to package instructions and cooled to room temperature. Warm the water and milk to 80°F (27°C) to optimize yeast activation.
2. Add Liquids to Bread Maker Pan: Pour the water and milk into the bread maker pan. Add the olive oil and honey.
3. Add Dry Ingredients: Sprinkle the salt over the liquid. Then, add the bread flour and whole wheat flour. Add the cooked quinoa and mixed seeds over the flours. Make a small indentation in the center of the dry ingredients (without reaching the wet) and add the yeast to this well.
4. Choose the Whole Wheat or Multigrain Cycle on your bread maker.
5. Start the Bread Maker: Close the lid and start the selected cycle. The bread maker will mix, knead, rise, and bake the Quinoa Multigrain Bread.
6. Cool Before Slicing: Once the cycle is complete, carefully remove the bread pan from the machine. Let the bread sit in the pan for about 10 minutes before turning it out onto a wire rack to cool completely.
7. Serve: Slice the bread once it has fully cooled. Quinoa Multigrain Bread is perfect for sandwiches, toasting, or simply enjoying with a spread of butter or your favorite jam

---

CHAPTER 02: MULTIGRAIN BREAD

Amaranth Multigrain Bread

Prep: 10   Min

Serves: 1 loaf (12 slices)

Ingredient:

- 1 cup + 2 tablespoons water (270 ml), 80°F (27°C)
- 1/4 cup milk (60 ml), 80°F (27°C)
- 2 tablespoons olive oil (30 ml)
- 2 tablespoons honey (42 g)
- 1½ teaspoons salt (8.54 g)
- 2 cups bread flour (254 g)
- 1 cup whole wheat flour (120 g)
- 1/2 cup amaranth flour (60 g) or cooked amaranth (if using cooked amaranth, reduce water by 1/4 cup)
- 1/4 cup mixed seeds (such as sunflower, flaxseed, or sesame seeds) (30 g)
- 1½ teaspoons active dry yeast (4.65 g)

Instruction:

1. Combine Liquids: Start by adding the water and milk to the bread maker pan. Then, incorporate the olive oil and honey.
2. Add Dry Ingredients: Sprinkle in the salt. Add the bread flour and whole wheat flour next. If using amaranth flour, add it now; if using cooked amaranth, remember to adjust the water as noted. Scatter the mixed seeds over the top.
3. Add Yeast: Make a small well in the center of the dry ingredients (but not so deep it reaches the liquid) and add the yeast.
4. Select the Cycle: Choose the Whole Wheat or Multigrain setting on your bread maker to accommodate the denser texture of the grains.
5. Start Baking: Close the lid and start the cycle. The machine will mix, knead, rise, and bake the Amaranth Multigrain Bread.
6. Cool Before Slicing: After the cycle finishes, carefully remove the bread pan from the machine. Let the bread cool in the pan for a few minutes before transferring it to a wire rack to cool completely.
7. Serve: Once cooled, slice the bread. It's perfect for sandwiches, toast, or to enjoy as is with your favorite spreads.

Millet Multigrain Bread

Prep: 10 Min

Serves: 1 loaf (12 slices)

Ingredient:

- 1 cup + 2 tablespoons water (270 ml), 80°F (27°C)
- 1/4 cup milk (60 ml), 80°F (27°C)
- 2 tablespoons olive oil (30 ml)
- 2 tablespoons honey (42 g)
- 1½ teaspoons salt (8.54 g)
- 2 cups bread flour (254 g)
- 1 cup whole wheat flour (120 g)
- 1/2 cup millet (uncooked) (90 g)
- 1/4 cup mixed seeds (such as sunflower seeds, flaxseeds, or sesame seeds) (30 g)
- 1½ teaspoons active dry yeast (4.65 g)

Instruction:

1. Add Liquids to Bread Maker Pan: Begin by adding the water and milk to the bread maker pan. Follow with the olive oil and honey.
2. Add Dry Ingredients: Next, sprinkle in the salt. Add the bread flour and whole wheat flour. Then, add the uncooked millet and the mixed seeds. Make a small indentation in the center of the dry ingredients (but not deep enough to reach the wet) and add the yeast to this well.
3. Select the Appropriate Cycle: Choose the Whole Wheat or Multigrain setting on your bread maker. This cycle is tailored for breads that include whole grains and seeds, providing enough time for kneading, rising, and baking.
4. Start the Bread Maker: Close the lid and start the cycle. The machine will take care of mixing, kneading, rising, and baking the Millet Multigrain Bread.
5. Cooling: Once the baking cycle is complete, carefully remove the bread pan from the machine. Let the bread sit in the pan for about 10 minutes before transferring it to a wire rack to cool completely.
6. Serve: Slice the cooled bread. This Millet Multigrain Bread is perfect for hearty sandwiches, toast, or to be enjoyed on its own with a spread of butter or jam.

CHAPTER 02: MULTIGRAIN BREAD

Chia Multigrain Bread

Prep: 10 Min

Serves: 1 loaf (12 slices)

Ingredient:

- 1 cup + 2 tablespoons water (270 ml), 80°F (27°C)
- 1/4 cup milk (60 ml), 80°F (27°C)
- 2 tablespoons olive oil (30 ml)
- 2 tablespoons honey (42 g)
- 1½ teaspoons salt (8.54 g)
- 2 cups bread flour (254 g)
- 1 cup whole wheat flour (120 g)
- 1/4 cup chia seeds (40 g)
- 1/4 cup mixed grains (such as quinoa, millet, and flaxseeds) (30 g)
- 1½ teaspoons active dry yeast (4.65 g)

Instruction:

1. Combine Liquids in Bread Maker Pan: Pour the water and milk into the bread maker pan. Follow with the olive oil and honey.
2. Add Dry Ingredients: Sprinkle the salt over the liquid. Add the bread flour and whole wheat flour. Then, distribute the chia seeds and mixed grains evenly over the flour. Make a small well in the center of the dry ingredients (without reaching the wet) and add the yeast to this well.
3. Select the Cycle: Choose the Whole Wheat or Multigrain setting on your bread maker to accommodate the denser dough mixture and ensure proper kneading and rising.
4. Start the Bread Maker: Close the lid and start the selected cycle. The machine will mix, knead, rise, and bake the Chia Multigrain Bread.
5. Cool Before Slicing: Once the cycle is complete, carefully remove the bread pan from the machine. Allow the bread to sit in the pan for about 10 minutes before transferring it to a wire rack to cool completely.
6. Serve: Slice the bread once it has fully cooled. Chia Multigrain Bread is ideal for hearty sandwiches, as toast with your favorite toppings, or simply enjoyed with butter

Flaxseed Multigrain Bread

Prep: 10 Min

Serves: 1 loaf (12 slices)

Ingredient:

- 1 cup + 2 tablespoons water (270 ml), 80°F (27°C)
- 1/4 cup milk (60 ml), 80°F (27°C)
- 2 tablespoons olive oil (30 ml)
- 2 tablespoons honey (42 g)
- 1½ teaspoons salt (8.54 g)
- 2 cups bread flour (254 g)
- 1 cup whole wheat flour (120 g)
- 1/4 cup ground flaxseed (30 g), plus extra for topping
- 1/4 cup mixed grains (such as oats, rye, and barley) (30 g)
- 1½ teaspoons active dry yeast (4.65 g)

 ## Instruction:

1. Prepare the Bread Maker Pan: Begin by adding the water and milk to the bread maker pan. Follow with the olive oil and honey.
2. Add the Dry Ingredients: Sprinkle in the salt. Then, add the bread flour and whole wheat flour. Add the ground flaxseed and mixed grains over the flours. Make a small well in the center of the dry ingredients (without reaching the wet) and add the yeast to this well.
3. Choose the Whole Wheat or Multigrain setting on your bread maker.
4. Close the lid and start the selected cycle. The machine will mix, knead, rise, and bake the Flaxseed Multigrain Bread.
5. Adding Flaxseed Topping: If your bread maker has a nut/fruit add-in signal, add some extra ground flaxseed at this time for a crunchy topping. If not, you can manually sprinkle ground flaxseed on the dough just before the final rise phase if your machine allows access.
6. Once the baking cycle is complete, carefully remove the bread pan from the machine. Let the bread cool in the pan for about 10 minutes, then transfer it to a wire rack to cool completely.
7. Slice the bread once cooled. Flaxseed Multigrain Bread is perfect for a nutritious breakfast toast, hearty sandwiches, or as a side to soups and salads.

CHAPTER 02: MULTIGRAIN BREAD

Pumpkin Seed Multigrain Bread

Prep: 10 Min

Serves: 1 loaf (12 slices)

Ingredient:

- 1 cup + 2 tablespoons water (270 ml), 80°F (27°C)
- 1/4 cup milk (60 ml), 80°F (27°C)
- 2 tablespoons olive oil (30 ml)
- 2 tablespoons honey (42 g)
- 1½ teaspoons salt (8.54 g)
- 2 cups bread flour (254 g)
- 1 cup whole wheat flour (120 g)
- 1/2 cup mixed grains (such as oats, barley, and rye) (60 g)
- 1/4 cup pumpkin seeds (30 g), plus extra for topping
- 1½ teaspoons active dry yeast (4.65 g)

 ## Instruction:

1. Combine Liquids in Bread Maker Pan: Pour the water and milk into the bread maker pan. Add the olive oil and honey.
2. Add Dry Ingredients: Sprinkle the salt over the liquid. Then, add the bread flour and whole wheat flour. Distribute the mixed grains and pumpkin seeds over the flours. Make a small well in the center of the dry ingredients (without reaching the wet) and add the yeast to this well.
3. Choose the Whole Wheat or Multigrain setting on your bread maker.
4. Close the lid and start the selected cycle. The machine will mix, knead, rise, and bake the Pumpkin Seed Multigrain Bread.
5. Add Pumpkin Seed Topping: If your bread maker has a nut/fruit add-in signal, add some extra pumpkin seeds at this time for a crunchy topping. If not, you might manually sprinkle pumpkin seeds on top of the dough just before the final rise phase, if your machine allows access.
6. Once the baking cycle is complete, carefully remove the bread pan from the machine. Let the bread sit in the pan for about 10 minutes before transferring it to a wire rack to cool completely.
7. Slice the bread once it has fully cooled. Pumpkin Seed Multigrain Bread is excellent for sandwiches, toast, or simply enjoyed with butter or cheese.

Khorasan Wheat (Kamut) Multigrain Bread

Prep: 10　Min

Serves: 1 loaf (12 slices)

Ingredient:

- 1 cup + 2 tablespoons water (270 ml), 80°F (27°C)
- 1/4 cup milk (60 ml), 80°F (27°C)
- 2 tablespoons olive oil (30 ml)
- 2 tablespoons honey (42 g)
- 1½ teaspoons salt (8.54 g)
- 1 ½ cups Kamut flour (Khorasan wheat flour) (180 g)
- 1 ½ cups bread flour (190 g)
- 1/2 cup multigrain mix (a combination of seeds and grains like flaxseed, sunflower seeds, oats, and barley) (60 g)
- 1½ teaspoons active dry yeast (4.65 g)

 ## Instruction:

1. Combine Liquids in Bread Maker Pan: Start by adding the water and milk to the bread maker pan. Then, incorporate the olive oil and honey.
2. Add Dry Ingredients: Sprinkle the salt over the liquid. Add both the Kamut flour and bread flour. Then, evenly distribute the multigrain mix over the flours. Make a small well in the center of the dry ingredients (but not deep enough to reach the wet) and add the yeast to this well.
3. Select the Appropriate Cycle: Choose the Whole Wheat or Multigrain setting on your bread maker, designed to handle the heavier dough made with whole grains and multigrain mixes.
4. Start the Bread Maker: Close the lid and start the selected cycle. The machine will mix, knead, rise, and bake the Khorasan Wheat Multigrain Bread.
5. Cool Before Slicing: Once the cycle is complete, carefully remove the bread pan from the machine. Allow the bread to sit in the pan for about 10 minutes before turning it out onto a wire rack to cool completely.
6. Serve: Slice the bread once it's fully cooled. Enjoy your Khorasan Wheat Multigrain Bread as a nutritious addition to any meal, perfect for sandwiches, toast, or simply with a spread of butter.

CHAPTER 02: MULTIGRAIN BREAD

Teff Multigrain Bread

Prep: 10　Min

Serves: 1 loaf (12 slices)

Ingredient:

- 1 cup + 2 tablespoons water (270 ml), 80°F (27°C)
- 1/4 cup milk (60 ml), 80°F (27°C)
- 2 tablespoons olive oil (30 ml)
- 2 tablespoons honey (42 g)
- 1½ teaspoons salt (8.54 g)
- 2 cups bread flour (254 g)
- 1 cup teff flour (120 g)
- 1/2 cup multigrain mix (including grains like quinoa, millet, and flaxseeds) (60 g)
- 1½ teaspoons active dry yeast (4.65 g)

 ## Instruction:

1. Prepare the Ingredients: Start by adding the water and milk to the bread maker pan. Follow with the olive oil and honey.
2. Add the Dry Ingredients: Next, sprinkle in the salt. Add the bread flour, followed by the teff flour. Then, distribute the multigrain mix evenly over the flours. Make a small well in the center of the dry ingredients (without reaching the wet) and add the yeast to this well.
3. Select the Appropriate Cycle: Choose the Whole Wheat or Multigrain setting on your bread maker. This cycle is designed for breads that include whole grains and heavier flours, providing the longer kneading and rising times needed.
4. Start the Bread Maker: Close the lid and start the selected cycle. The machine will mix, knead, rise, and bake the Teff Multigrain Bread.
5. Cool Before Slicing: Once the cycle is complete, carefully remove the bread pan from the machine. Let the bread sit in the pan for about 10 minutes before turning it out onto a wire rack to cool completely.
6. Serve: Slice the bread once it has fully cooled. Teff Multigrain Bread is perfect for a nutritious breakfast, hearty sandwiches, or as a complement to your favorite spreads.

Multigrain Baguette (a twist on the classic French bread)

Prep: 20 Min

Serves: 2 medium baguettes

Ingredient:

- 1 ½ cups water (360 ml), 80°F (27°C)
- 1 tablespoon olive oil (15 ml)
- 1 tablespoon honey (21 g)
- 1 ½ teaspoons salt (8.54 g)
- 2 cups bread flour (254 g)
- 1 cup whole wheat flour (120 g)
- ½ cup multigrain mix (such as rye flour, finely ground cornmeal, oats, and flaxseeds) (60 g)
- 1 tablespoon mixed seeds (such as sesame, poppy, and sunflower seeds) for the dough, plus extra for topping
- 2 teaspoons active dry yeast (6.2 g)

 ## Instruction:

1. Pour the water into the bread maker pan. Add the olive oil and honey. Then, sprinkle in the salt.
2. Add the bread flour, whole wheat flour, and your multigrain mix. Distribute the 1 tablespoon of mixed seeds throughout the flour. Make a small well in the center of the flour (but not deep enough to reach the liquid) and add the yeast.
3. Select the Dough cycle on your bread maker and start it. The machine will mix, knead, and rise the dough.
4. Shape the Baguettes: Once the dough cycle is complete, gently remove the dough onto a lightly floured surface. Divide the dough in half.
5. Shape each half into a long, thin loaf, about 14 inches long. Place on a baguette pan or a baking sheet lined with parchment paper.
6. Second Rise: Cover the shaped baguettes with a clean kitchen towel. Let them rise in a warm place until nearly doubled in size, about 30-45 minutes.
7. Preheat your oven to 450°F (232°C). Just before baking, make several diagonal slashes on each baguette with a sharp knife. Optionally, mist the baguettes with water and sprinkle additional mixed seeds on top.
8. Place the baguettes in the oven. Bake for 20-25 minutes, or until the baguettes are golden brown and sound hollow when tapped on the bottom. Remove the baguettes from the oven and let them cool on a wire rack before slicing.

CHAPTER 02: MULTIGRAIN BREAD

Ancient Grains Multigrain Bread

Prep: 10 Min

Serves: 1 loaf (12 slices)

Ingredient:

- 1 cup + 2 tablespoons water (270 ml), 80°F (27°C)
- 1/4 cup milk (60 ml), 80°F (27°C)
- 2 tablespoons olive oil (30 ml)
- 2 tablespoons honey (42 g)
- 1½ teaspoons salt (8.54 g)
- 1 cup einkorn flour (120 g)
- 1 cup emmer flour (120 g)
- 1 cup bread flour (120 g) - to help with the rise, as ancient grains have different gluten structures
- 1/4 cup mixed seeds (such as flaxseed, sunflower seeds, and sesame seeds) (30 g)
- 1½ teaspoons active dry yeast (4.65 g)

 ## Instruction:

1. Combine Liquids in Bread Maker Pan: Start by adding the water and milk to the bread maker pan. Follow with the olive oil and honey.
2. Add the Dry Ingredients: Next, sprinkle in the salt. Add the einkorn flour, emmer flour, and bread flour. Then, evenly distribute the mixed seeds over the flours. Make a small well in the center of the dry ingredients (without reaching the wet) and add the yeast to this well.
3. Select the Appropriate Cycle: Choose the Whole Wheat or Multigrain setting on your bread maker. This cycle is tailored for breads that include whole grains and seeds, providing longer kneading and rising times needed for dense dough.
4. Start the Bread Maker: Close the lid and start the selected cycle. The machine will mix, knead, rise, and bake the Ancient Grains Multigrain Bread.
5. Cool Before Slicing: Once the cycle is complete, carefully remove the bread pan from the machine. Let the bread cool in the pan for about 10 minutes before turning it out onto a wire rack to cool completely.
6. Serve: Slice the bread once it has fully cooled. Enjoy your Ancient Grains Multigrain Bread as a nutritious addition to any meal, perfect for sandwiches, toast, or simply with a spread of butter.

Cheddar Cheese Bread

Prep: 10 Min

Serves: 1 loaf (12 slices)

Ingredient:

- 1 cup + 2 tablespoons water (270 ml), 80°F (27°C)
- 2 tablespoons olive oil (30 ml)
- 1½ teaspoons salt (8.54 g)
- 3 cups bread flour (381 g)
- 1½ teaspoons sugar (6.3 g) - adjusted for clarity
- 1½ cups shredded cheddar cheese (150 g)
- 2 teaspoons active dry yeast (6.2 g)

 ## Instruction:

1. Add Liquids: Pour the water into the bread maker pan. Add the olive oil.
2. Add Dry Ingredients: Next, add the salt, followed by the bread flour. Sprinkle the sugar evenly over the flour.
3. Add Cheese: Distribute the shredded cheddar cheese evenly over the flour. This helps to ensure that the cheese is well incorporated throughout the dough.
4. Add Yeast: Make a small well in the center of the dry ingredients (ensuring it doesn't reach the wet layer) and add the yeast.
5. Select the Cycle: Choose the Basic or White Bread setting on your bread maker.
6. Close the lid and start the machine. The bread maker will mix, knead, rise, and bake the Cheddar Cheese Bread.
7. Once the cycle is complete, carefully remove the bread pan from the machine. Let the bread sit in the pan for about 5-10 minutes before turning it out onto a wire rack to cool completely. This makes slicing easier and helps to finalize the bread's structure.
8. Slice the bread and enjoy! Cheddar Cheese Bread is delicious when served warm, offering a melty and savory cheese flavor that's perfect as a side to soups, salads, or enjoyed on its own.

CHAPTER 03: CHEESE BREAD

Parmesan Garlic Bread

Prep: 10 Min

Serves: 1 loaf (12 slices)

Ingredient:

- 1 cup + 2 tablespoons water (270 ml), 80°F (27°C)
- 2 tablespoons olive oil (30 ml)
- 1½ teaspoons salt (8.54 g)
- 3 cups bread flour (381 g)
- 2 tablespoons sugar (25.2 g)
- 1½ teaspoons active dry yeast (4.65 g)
- 1/2 cup grated Parmesan cheese (50 g)
- 2 teaspoons garlic powder (5.2 g) or 2 tablespoons finely minced fresh garlic (30 ml)

Instruction:

1. Prepare the Ingredients: Begin by adding the water and olive oil to the bread maker pan.
2. Add Dry Ingredients: Sprinkle the salt and sugar into the pan. Then, add the bread flour. Make a small well in the center of the flour and add the active dry yeast.
3. Add Flavorings: Distribute the grated Parmesan cheese and garlic powder or minced garlic evenly over the flour. If using fresh garlic, ensure it's finely minced to distribute the flavor evenly.
4. Select the Cycle: Choose the Basic or White Bread setting on your bread maker. This cycle is suitable for achieving a soft texture with a nicely browned crust.
5. Start the Bread Maker: Close the lid and start the machine. The bread maker will mix, knead, rise, and bake the Parmesan Garlic Bread.
6. Cool Before Slicing: Once the baking cycle is complete, carefully remove the bread pan from the machine. Let the bread cool in the pan for about 5-10 minutes before turning it out onto a wire rack to cool completely.
7. Serve: Slice the bread and enjoy! Parmesan Garlic Bread is fantastic served warm, making it a perfect accompaniment to pasta dishes, soups, or salads.

Mozzarella and Herb Bread

Prep: 10   Min

Serves: 1 loaf (12 slices)

Ingredient:

- 1 cup + 2 tablespoons water (270 ml), 80°F (27°C)
- 2 tablespoons olive oil (30 ml)
- 1½ teaspoons salt (8.54 g)
- 3 cups bread flour (381 g)
- 1½ teaspoons sugar (6.3 g) - adjusted for clarity
- 1 cup shredded mozzarella cheese (100 g)
- 1 tablespoon dried Italian herbs (basil, oregano, rosemary mix) (3 g)
- 2 teaspoons active dry yeast (6.2 g)

 ## Instruction:

1. Add Liquids to Bread Maker Pan: Pour the water into the bread maker pan. Add the olive oil.
2. Add Dry Ingredients: Next, add the salt and sugar. Then, add the bread flour. Sprinkle the dried Italian herbs over the flour.
3. Add Cheese: Distribute the shredded mozzarella cheese evenly over the top. Make a small well in the center of the dry ingredients (ensuring it doesn't reach the wet layer) and add the yeast.
4. Select the Cycle: Choose the Basic or White Bread setting on your bread maker. This cycle is suitable for cheese bread as it provides the right balance of kneading, rising, and baking.
5. Start the Bread Maker: Close the lid and start the machine. The bread maker will mix, knead, rise, and bake the Mozzarella and Herb Bread.
6. Once the cycle is complete, carefully remove the bread pan from the machine. Let the bread sit in the pan for about 5-10 minutes before turning it out onto a wire rack to cool completely.
7. Slice the bread and enjoy! Mozzarella and Herb Bread is delicious when served warm, offering a melty and savory cheese flavor that's perfect as a side to pasta, soups, or salads.

CHAPTER 03: CHEESE BREAD

Gouda and Onion Bread

Prep: 10   Min

Serves: 1 loaf (12 slices)

Ingredient:

- 1 cup + 2 tablespoons water (270 ml), 80°F (27°C)
- 2 tablespoons olive oil (30 ml)
- 1½ teaspoons salt (8.54 g)
- 3 cups bread flour (381 g)
- 1 tablespoon sugar (12.6 g)
- 1 cup shredded Gouda cheese (100 g)
- 1/2 cup finely chopped onion (about 80 g)
- 2 teaspoons active dry yeast (6.2 g)

 ## Instruction:

1. Prepare the Ingredients: Start by adding the water to the bread maker pan. Follow with the olive oil.
2. Add Dry Ingredients: Sprinkle the salt and sugar into the pan. Then, add the bread flour. Make a small well in the center of the flour and add the active dry yeast.
3. Add Cheese and Onion: Distribute the shredded Gouda cheese and finely chopped onion evenly over the flour. If your bread maker has a mix-in feature, add the onions and cheese at the signal; otherwise, add them at the beginning to ensure they are well incorporated into the dough.
4. Select the Cycle: Choose the Basic or White Bread setting on your bread maker.
5. Start the Bread Maker: Close the lid and start the machine. The bread maker will mix, knead, rise, and bake the Gouda and Onion Bread.
6. Cool Before Slicing: Once the baking cycle is complete, carefully remove the bread pan from the machine. Allow the bread to sit in the pan for about 5-10 minutes before turning it out onto a wire rack to cool completely.
7. Slice the bread and enjoy! Gouda and Onion Bread is perfect served warm, allowing the Gouda cheese to be slightly melted and the onion flavor to be pronounced.

Asiago Cheese Bread

Prep: 10 Min

Serves: 1 loaf (12 slices)

Ingredient:

- 1 cup + 2 tablespoons water (270 ml), 80°F (27°C)
- 2 tablespoons olive oil (30 ml)
- 1½ teaspoons salt (8.54 g)
- 3 cups bread flour (381 g)
- 2 tablespoons sugar (25.2 g)
- 1½ cups shredded Asiago cheese (150 g), plus extra for topping
- 1½ teaspoons active dry yeast (4.65 g)

 ## Instruction:

1. Add Liquids to Bread Maker Pan: Begin by pouring the water into the bread maker pan. Add the olive oil.
2. Add Dry Ingredients: Next, sprinkle the salt and sugar over the liquid. Add the bread flour. Ensure the Asiago cheese is shredded and evenly distribute it over the flour. Make a small well in the center of the dry ingredients (without touching the wet ingredients) and add the yeast.
3. Choose the Basic or White Bread setting on your bread maker.
4. Close the lid and start the machine. The bread maker will mix, knead, rise, and bake the Asiago Cheese Bread.
5. If your bread maker has a nut/fruit add-in signal, add some extra shredded Asiago cheese at this time for a cheesy crust. If not, you can manually add Asiago cheese on top of the dough just before the final rise phase, if your machine allows access.
6. Once the baking cycle is complete, carefully remove the bread pan from the machine. Let the bread cool in the pan for about 5-10 minutes before turning it out onto a wire rack to cool completely.
7. Slice the bread and enjoy! Asiago Cheese Bread is delicious when served warm, offering a melty and savory cheese flavor that's perfect as a side to any meal or enjoyed on its own.

CHAPTER 03: CHEESE BREAD

Feta and Spinach Bread

Prep: 15 Min

Serves: 1 loaf (12 slices)

Ingredient:

- 1 cup + 2 tablespoons water (270 ml), 80°F (27°C)
- 2 tablespoons olive oil (30 ml)
- 1½ teaspoons salt (8.54 g)
- 3 cups bread flour (381 g)
- 1 tablespoon sugar (12.6 g)
- 1½ cups fresh spinach, finely chopped (about 40 g after chopping)
- 1 cup crumbled feta cheese (150 g)
- 2 teaspoons active dry yeast (6.2 g)

Instruction:

1. Prepare the Spinach: Rinse the spinach leaves and chop them finely. Squeeze out any excess moisture with a clean towel or paper towels to prevent the bread from becoming too wet.
2. Add Liquids to Bread Maker Pan: Begin by pouring the water into the bread maker pan. Add the olive oil.
3. Add Dry Ingredients: Next, sprinkle the salt and sugar over the liquid. Then, add the bread flour. Make a small well in the center of the dry ingredients (without touching the wet ingredients) and add the yeast.
4. Add Spinach and Feta: Distribute the finely chopped spinach and crumbled feta cheese evenly over the flour. If your bread maker has a mix-in feature, add them at the beep signal; otherwise, add them from the start to ensure they're well incorporated into the dough.
5. Choose the Basic or White Bread setting on your bread maker.
6. Close the lid and start the machine. The bread maker will mix, knead, rise, and bake the Feta and Spinach Bread.
7. Once the baking cycle is complete, carefully remove the bread pan from the machine. Let the bread sit in the pan for about 5-10 minutes before turning it out onto a wire rack to cool completely.
8. Slice the bread and enjoy!

Blue Cheese and Walnut Bread

Prep: 10 Min

Serves: 1 loaf (12 slices)

Ingredient:

- 1 cup + 2 tablespoons water (270 ml), 80°F (27°C)
- 2 tablespoons olive oil (30 ml)
- 1½ teaspoons salt (8.54 g)
- 3 cups bread flour (381 g)
- 1 tablespoon sugar (12.6 g)
- ¾ cup crumbled blue cheese (75 g)
- ¾ cup chopped walnuts (75 g)
- 2 teaspoons active dry yeast (6.2 g)

Instruction:

1. Add Liquids to Bread Maker Pan: Begin by pouring the water and olive oil into the bread maker pan.
2. Add Dry Ingredients: Sprinkle in the salt and sugar. Add the bread flour next. Create a small well in the center of the dry ingredients and add the yeast to this well.
3. Add Blue Cheese and Walnuts: Evenly distribute the crumbled blue cheese and chopped walnuts over the flour. If your bread maker has a mix-in feature, use it accordingly; otherwise, add them with the other ingredients before starting the cycle.
4. Select the Cycle: Set your bread maker to the Basic or White Bread cycle.
5. Start the Bread Maker: Close the lid and start the machine. It will mix, knead, rise, and bake the bread.
6. Cool Before Slicing: After the cycle completes, remove the bread pan from the machine. Allow the bread to sit for a few minutes before transferring it to a wire rack to cool completely.
7. Serve: Once cooled, slice the bread and serve.

CHAPTER 03: CHEESE BREAD

Swiss Cheese and Mushroom Bread

Prep: 20 Min

Serves: 1 loaf (12 slices)

Ingredient:

- 1 cup + 2 tablespoons water (270 ml), 80°F (27°C)
- 2 tablespoons olive oil (30 ml)
- 1½ teaspoons salt (8.54 g)
- 3 cups bread flour (381 g)
- 1½ teaspoons sugar (6.3 g) — Adjusted to match your conversion request
- 1 cup finely chopped mushrooms (about 70 g) — Sautéed and cooled
- 1 cup shredded Swiss cheese (about 100 g)
- 1½ teaspoons active dry yeast (4.65 g)

Instruction:

1. Sauté Mushrooms: Before adding them to the bread maker, sauté the mushrooms in a little olive oil until they're golden and most of their moisture has evaporated. Let them cool to room temperature.
2. Add Liquids to Bread Maker Pan: Pour the water and olive oil into the bread maker pan.
3. Add Dry Ingredients: Add the salt, sugar, and bread flour to the pan. Make a small well in the center of the flour and add the yeast to this well.
4. Add Cheese and Mushrooms: Distribute the cooled, sautéed mushrooms and shredded Swiss cheese evenly over the flour. If your bread maker has a mix-in feature, use it according to the manufacturer's instructions; otherwise, add them at the beginning.
5. Set your bread maker to the Basic or White Bread setting.
6. Close the lid and start the cycle. The machine will take care of the rest, mixing the ingredients, kneading the dough, letting it rise, and baking it to perfection.
7. Once the cycle is complete, carefully remove the bread pan from the machine. Allow the bread to cool in the pan for about 10 minutes before transferring it to a wire rack to cool completely.
8. Slice the Swiss Cheese and Mushroom Bread and enjoy.

Provolone and Olive Bread

Prep: 10 Min

Serves: 1 loaf (12 slices)

Ingredient:

- 1 cup + 2 tablespoons water (270 ml), 80°F (27°C)
- 2 tablespoons olive oil (30 ml)
- 1½ teaspoons salt (8.54 g)
- 3 cups bread flour (381 g)
- 1 tablespoon sugar (12.6 g)
- 1 cup shredded Provolone cheese (100 g)
- ½ cup chopped olives (green, black, or a mix) (about 75 g, drained if using canned)
- 1½ teaspoons active dry yeast (4.65 g)

 ## Instruction:

1. Prepare the Bread Maker: Pour the water and olive oil into the bread maker pan.
2. Add Dry Ingredients: Sprinkle the salt and sugar over the liquid. Then, add the bread flour. Make a small well in the center of the flour and add the yeast.
3. Add Cheese and Olives: Distribute the shredded Provolone cheese and chopped olives evenly over the flour. If your bread maker has a mix-in feature, use it accordingly; otherwise, add them with the other ingredients before starting the cycle.
4. Select the Cycle: Choose the Basic or White Bread setting on your bread maker.
5. Start the Bread Maker: Close the lid and start the machine. It will mix, knead, rise, and bake the Provolone and Olive Bread.
6. Cooling: After the baking cycle completes, carefully remove the bread pan from the machine. Let the bread sit in the pan for a few minutes before transferring it to a wire rack to cool completely.
7. Serve: Once cooled, slice the bread and serve. This Provolone and Olive Bread brings a delightful combination of flavors, making it perfect for sandwiches or to enjoy on its own as a savory treat.

CHAPTER 03: CHEESE BREAD

Brie and Cranberry Bread

Prep: 10 Min

Serves: 1 loaf (12 slices)

Ingredient:

- 1 cup + 2 tablespoons water (270 ml), 80°F (27°C)
- 2 tablespoons olive oil (30 ml)
- 1½ teaspoons salt (8.54 g)
- 3 cups bread flour (381 g)
- 1 tablespoon sugar (12.6 g)
- ¾ cup diced Brie cheese (remove rind) (100 g)
- ¾ cup dried cranberries (90 g)
- 1½ teaspoons active dry yeast (4.65 g)

 ## Instruction:

1. Add Liquids to Bread Maker Pan: Begin by pouring the water into the bread maker pan. Follow with the olive oil.
2. Add Dry Ingredients: Next, sprinkle in the salt and sugar. Then, add the bread flour. Make a small well in the center of the dry ingredients (without touching the wet ingredients) and add the yeast.
3. Add Brie and Cranberries: Evenly distribute the diced Brie and dried cranberries over the flour. If your bread maker has a mix-in feature, use it to add the Brie and cranberries at the signal; otherwise, add them at the beginning to ensure they're well incorporated.
4. Select the Cycle: Choose the Basic or White Bread setting on your bread maker.
5. Close the lid and start the machine. The bread maker will mix, knead, rise, and bake the Brie and Cranberry Bread.
6. Once the baking cycle is complete, carefully remove the bread pan from the machine. Let the bread cool in the pan for about 5-10 minutes before turning it out onto a wire rack to cool completely.
7. Slice the bread and enjoy! Brie and Cranberry Bread is delightful when served warm, allowing the Brie to slightly melt and mingle with the sweet-tart cranberries.

Cream Cheese and Jalapeño Bread

Prep: 10　Min

Serves: 1 loaf (12 slices)

Ingredient:

- 1 cup + 2 tablespoons water (270 ml), 80°F (27°C)
- 2 tablespoons olive oil (30 ml)
- 1½ teaspoons salt (8.54 g)
- 3 cups bread flour (381 g)
- 1 tablespoon sugar (12.6 g)
- ¾ cup cream cheese, cut into small cubes (about 170 g)
- 2 to 3 medium jalapeños, finely chopped (adjust to taste), seeds removed for less heat (about 30 to 45 g)
- 1½ teaspoons active dry yeast (4.65 g)

 ## Instruction:

1. Prepare the Ingredients: Start by adding the water and olive oil to the bread maker pan.
2. Add Dry Ingredients: Sprinkle in the salt and sugar. Then, add the bread flour. Make a small well in the center of the flour and add the yeast.
3. Add Cream Cheese and Jalapeños: Distribute the cubes of cream cheese and the chopped jalapeños evenly over the flour. If your bread maker has a mix-in feature, use it to add the cream cheese and jalapeños at the signal; otherwise, add them at the beginning to ensure they're well incorporated.
4. Select the Cycle: Choose the Basic or White Bread setting on your bread maker.
5. Close the lid and start the machine. The bread maker will mix, knead, rise, and bake the Cream Cheese and Jalapeño Bread.
6. Once the baking cycle is complete, carefully remove the bread pan from the machine. Let the bread cool in the pan for about 5-10 minutes before turning it out onto a wire rack to cool completely.
7. Slice the bread and enjoy! Cream Cheese and Jalapeño Bread offers a deliciously creamy and spicy flavor, perfect as a unique side dish or for making standout sandwiches.

CHAPTER 03: CHEESE BREAD

Gruyère and Thyme Bread

Prep: 10　Min

Serves: 1 loaf (12 slices)

Ingredient:

- 1 cup + 2 tablespoons water (270 ml), 80°F (27°C)
- 2 tablespoons olive oil (30 ml)
- 1½ teaspoons salt (8.54 g)
- 3 cups bread flour (381 g)
- 1 tablespoon sugar (12.6 g)
- 1 cup grated Gruyère cheese (100 g)
- 2 tablespoons fresh thyme leaves (or 2 teaspoons dried thyme) (6 g if fresh, 2 g if dried)
- 1½ teaspoons active dry yeast (4.65 g)

 ## Instruction:

1. Add Liquids to Bread Maker Pan: Begin by pouring the water into the bread maker pan. Add the olive oil.
2. Add Dry Ingredients: Sprinkle the salt and sugar over the liquid. Then, add the bread flour. Make a small well in the center of the dry ingredients (without touching the wet ingredients) and add the yeast.
3. Add Cheese and Thyme: Evenly distribute the grated Gruyère cheese and thyme leaves over the flour. If your bread maker has a mix-in feature, use it to add the cheese and thyme at the beep signal; otherwise, add them at the beginning to ensure they're well incorporated.
4. Select the Cycle: Choose the Basic or White Bread setting on your bread maker.
5. Close the lid and start the machine. It will mix, knead, rise, and bake the Gruyère and Thyme Bread.
6. After the baking cycle completes, carefully remove the bread pan from the machine. Let the bread cool in the pan for a few minutes before transferring it to a wire rack to cool completely.
7. Slice the bread and enjoy. Gruyère and Thyme Bread pairs wonderfully with soups, salads, or can be enjoyed on its own, highlighting the rich flavors of the cheese and the aromatic thyme.

Ricotta and Lemon Zest Bread

Prep: 10   Min

Serves: 1 loaf (12 slices)

Ingredient:

- 1 cup + 2 tablespoons water (270 ml), 80°F (27°C)
- 1 cup ricotta cheese (245 g), room temperature
- 2 tablespoons olive oil (30 ml)
- 1½ teaspoons salt (8.54 g)
- 2 tablespoons sugar (25.2 g)
- 3 cups bread flour (381 g)
- Zest of 2 lemons (use a grater to get fine zest, approximately 2 tablespoons or 6 g)
- 1½ teaspoons active dry yeast (4.65 g)

 ## Instruction:

1. Add Liquids First: Pour the water into the bread maker pan. Add the olive oil and ricotta cheese. Ensure the ricotta is at room temperature to blend smoothly with other ingredients.
2. Add Dry Ingredients: Sprinkle in the salt and sugar. Then, add the bread flour. Spread the lemon zest evenly over the flour. Make a small well in the center of the flour (not too deep) and add the yeast to this well.
3. Select the Cycle: Choose the Basic or White Bread cycle on your bread maker.
4. Start the Bread Maker: Close the lid and start the selected cycle. The bread maker will take care of mixing, kneading, rising, and baking the Ricotta and Lemon Zest Bread.
5. Cool Before Slicing: Once the baking cycle is complete, carefully remove the bread pan from the machine. Let the bread sit in the pan for about 5-10 minutes before turning it out onto a wire rack to cool completely.
6. Serve: Slice the bread once cooled. This Ricotta and Lemon Zest Bread is wonderfully aromatic with a light, fluffy texture, making it a perfect companion to your morning coffee or tea, or as an accompaniment to salads and soups.

CHAPTER 03: CHEESE BREAD

Pepper Jack and Corn Bread

Prep: 10   Min

Serves: 1 loaf (12 slices)

Ingredient:

- 1 cup lukewarm water (240 ml), 80°F (27°C)
- 2 tablespoons olive oil (30 ml)
- 1½ teaspoons salt (8.54 g)
- 3 cups bread flour (381 g)
- 1 cup cornmeal (about 120 g) - This will give the bread its distinct corn flavor and texture.
- 2 tablespoons sugar (25.2 g) - Adjusts for the sweetness typically found in cornbread.
- 1 cup grated Pepper Jack cheese (about 100 g) - Adds a spicy, creamy element to the bread.
- ½ cup canned corn (drained) or frozen corn (thawed) (about 85 g) - Incorporates actual corn kernels for added texture and flavor.
- 1½ teaspoons active dry yeast (4.65 g)

Instruction:

1. Prepare the Bread Maker: Begin by adding the water and olive oil to the bread maker pan.
2. Add Dry Ingredients: Add the salt, sugar, bread flour, and cornmeal to the pan, layering them evenly. This combination of flour and cornmeal creates a balanced texture that's neither too dense nor too crumbly.
3. Add Cheese and Corn: Sprinkle the grated Pepper Jack cheese and corn over the dry ingredients. These ingredients will be mixed into the dough during the kneading process, distributing the spicy cheese flavor and corn throughout the bread.
4. Add Yeast: Make a small well in the center of the dry ingredients (not too deep) and add the yeast. Ensuring the yeast does not come into direct contact with the salt or liquid ingredients immediately helps protect its activity until kneading begins.
5. Choose the Basic or White Bread setting on your bread maker.
6. Close the lid and start the selected cycle. The machine will mix, knead, rise, and bake the Pepper Jack and Corn Bread.
7. Once the baking cycle is complete, carefully remove the bread pan from the machine. Let the bread cool in the pan for about 10 minutes before transferring it to a wire rack to cool completely.
8. Slice the Pepper Jack and Corn Bread and enjoy. It pairs wonderfully with chili, soups, or can be enjoyed on its own as a spicy, savory snack.

Havarti and Dill Bread

Prep: 10 Min

Serves: 1 loaf (12 slices)

Ingredient:

- 1 cup + 2 tablespoons water (270 ml), 80°F (27°C)
- 2 tablespoons olive oil (30 ml)
- 1½ teaspoons salt (8.54 g)
- 3 cups bread flour (381 g)
- 1 tablespoon sugar (12.6 g)
- 1 cup grated Havarti cheese (100 g)
- 2 tablespoons fresh dill, chopped (or 2 teaspoons dried dill) (6 g if fresh, 2 g if dried)
- 1½ teaspoons active dry yeast (4.65 g)

 ## Instruction:

1. Prepare the Bread Maker: Start by adding the water and olive oil to the bread maker pan.
2. Add Dry Ingredients: Next, sprinkle in the salt and sugar. Then, add the bread flour. Make a small well in the center of the flour and add the yeast.
3. Add Cheese and Dill: Distribute the grated Havarti cheese and dill evenly over the flour. If your bread maker has a mix-in feature, use it to add the cheese and dill at the beep signal; otherwise, add them at the beginning to ensure they're well incorporated.
4. Select the Cycle: Choose the Basic or White Bread setting on your bread maker.
5. Start the Bread Maker: Close the lid and start the machine. The bread maker will mix, knead, rise, and bake the Havarti and Dill Bread.
6. Once the baking cycle is complete, carefully remove the bread pan from the machine. Let the bread sit in the pan for about 5-10 minutes before turning it out onto a wire rack to cool completely.
7. Slice the bread and enjoy! Havarti and Dill Bread is delicious when served warm, offering a creamy and aromatic flavor that's perfect as a side to any meal or enjoyed on its own.

CHAPTER 03: CHEESE BREAD

Goat Cheese and Sun-Dried Tomato Bread

Prep: 10 Min

Serves: 1 loaf (12 slices)

Ingredient:

- 1 cup + 2 tablespoons water (270 ml), 80°F (27°C)
- 2 tablespoons olive oil (30 ml)
- 1½ teaspoons salt (8.54 g)
- 3 cups bread flour (381 g)
- 1 tablespoon sugar (12.6 g)
- ¾ cup crumbled goat cheese (75 g)
- ¾ cup chopped sun-dried tomatoes (not in oil) (75 g), if using sun-dried tomatoes in oil, drain them well.
- 1½ teaspoons active dry yeast (4.65 g)

 ## Instruction:

1. Prepare the Bread Maker: Begin by adding the water and olive oil to the bread maker pan.
2. Add Dry Ingredients: Sprinkle in the salt and sugar. Then, add the bread flour. Make a small well in the center of the flour and add the yeast.
3. Add Goat Cheese and Sun-Dried Tomatoes: Distribute the crumbled goat cheese and chopped sun-dried tomatoes evenly over the flour. If your bread maker has a mix-in feature, use it to add the cheese and tomatoes at the beep signal; otherwise, add them at the beginning to ensure they're well incorporated.
4. Select the Cycle: Choose the Basic or White Bread setting on your bread maker.
5. Start the Bread Maker: Close the lid and start the machine. The bread maker will mix, knead, rise, and bake the Goat Cheese and Sun-Dried Tomato Bread.
6. Cool Before Slicing: Once the baking cycle is complete, carefully remove the bread pan from the machine. Let the bread cool in the pan for about 5-10 minutes before turning it out onto a wire rack to cool completely.
7. Serve: Slice the bread and enjoy! Goat Cheese and Sun-Dried Tomato Bread is exceptionally flavorful, perfect for serving with a salad, as part of a cheese board, or simply enjoying on its own.

Colby and Bacon Bread

Prep: 15 Min

Serves: 1 loaf (12 slices)

Ingredient:

- 1 cup + 2 tablespoons water (270 ml), 80°F (27°C)
- 2 tablespoons olive oil (30 ml)
- 1½ teaspoons salt (8.54 g)
- 3 cups bread flour (381 g)
- 1 tablespoon sugar (12.6 g)
- ¾ cup grated Colby cheese (75 g)
- ½ cup cooked, crumbled bacon (about 4 slices or 60 g)
- 1½ teaspoons active dry yeast (4.65 g)

 ## Instruction:

1. Prepare the Ingredients: Begin by adding the water and olive oil to the bread maker pan.
2. Add Dry Ingredients: Sprinkle the salt and sugar over the liquid. Then, add the bread flour. Make a small well in the center of the flour and add the yeast.
3. Add Cheese and Bacon: Evenly distribute the grated Colby cheese and crumbled bacon over the flour. If your bread maker has a mix-in feature, add them at the beep signal; otherwise, add them at the beginning to ensure they're well incorporated into the dough.
4. Select the Cycle: Choose the Basic or White Bread setting on your bread maker.
5. Close the lid and start the machine. The bread maker will mix, knead, rise, and bake the Colby and Bacon Bread.
6. Once the baking cycle is complete, carefully remove the bread pan from the machine. Let the bread cool in the pan for about 5-10 minutes before turning it out onto a wire rack to cool completely.
7. Slice the bread and enjoy! Colby and Bacon Bread is delicious when served warm, offering a savory and satisfying flavor that's perfect for breakfast, as a sandwich base, or as a side to your favorite dishes.

CHAPTER 03: CHEESE BREAD

Manchego and Quince Paste Bread

Prep: 10 Min

Serves: 1 loaf (12 slices)

Ingredient:

- 1 cup + 2 tablespoons water (270 ml), 80°F (27°C)
- 2 tablespoons olive oil (30 ml)
- 1½ teaspoons salt (8.54 g)
- 3 cups bread flour (381 g)
- 1 tablespoon sugar (12.6 g)
- 1 cup grated Manchego cheese (about 100 g)
- ½ cup diced quince paste (about 120 g)
- 1½ teaspoons active dry yeast (4.65 g)

Instruction:

1. Prepare Ingredients: Grate the Manchego cheese and dice the quince paste into small pieces. This ensures even distribution throughout the bread.
2. Layer Wet Ingredients in Pan: Pour the water and olive oil into the bread maker pan.
3. Add Dry Ingredients: Add the salt, sugar, and bread flour to the pan. Make a small well in the center of the flour and add the yeast.
4. Add Cheese and Quince Paste: Sprinkle the grated Manchego cheese and diced quince paste over the flour. If your bread maker has an add-in feature, use it according to the manufacturer's instructions; otherwise, add them on top of the flour before starting the cycle.
5. Choose the Basic or White Bread Cycle on your bread maker.
6. Close the lid and start the cycle. The machine will mix the ingredients, knead the dough, let it rise, and bake it to perfection.
7. Once the baking cycle is complete, carefully remove the bread pan from the machine. Let the bread cool in the pan for about 10 minutes before transferring it to a wire rack to cool completely.
8. Slice the Manchego and Quince Paste Bread and enjoy. This bread is especially delicious served with a bit of olive oil, or simply on its own to savor the unique flavors.

Edam and Roasted Red Pepper Bread

Prep: 10   Min

Serves: 1 loaf (12 slices)

Ingredient:

- 1 cup + 2 tablespoons water (270 ml), 80°F (27°C)
- 2 tablespoons olive oil (30 ml)
- 1½ teaspoons salt (8.54 g)
- 3 cups bread flour (381 g)
- 1 tablespoon sugar (12.6 g)
- ¾ cup grated Edam cheese (75 g)
- ½ cup roasted red peppers, drained and chopped (about 75 g)
- 1½ teaspoons active dry yeast (4.65 g)

 ## Instruction:

1. Prepare the Ingredients: Start by adding the water and olive oil to the bread maker pan.
2. Add Dry Ingredients: Sprinkle in the salt and sugar. Then, add the bread flour. Make a small well in the center of the flour and add the yeast.
3. Add Cheese and Red Peppers: Distribute the grated Edam cheese and chopped roasted red peppers evenly over the flour. If your bread maker has a mix-in feature, add them at the beep signal; otherwise, add them at the beginning to ensure they're well incorporated into the dough.
4. Choose the Basic or White Bread setting on your bread maker.
5. Close the lid and start the machine. The bread maker will mix, knead, rise, and bake the Edam and Roasted Red Pepper Bread.
6. Once the baking cycle is complete, carefully remove the bread pan from the machine. Let the bread cool in the pan for about 5-10 minutes before turning it out onto a wire rack to cool completely.
7. Slice the bread and enjoy! Edam and Roasted Red Pepper Bread is delicious when served warm, offering a delightful combination of flavors that complement each other perfectly.

CHAPTER 03: CHEESE BREAD

Camembert and Apple Bread

Prep: 15   Min

Serves: 1 loaf (12 slices)

Ingredient:

- 1 cup + 2 tablespoons water (270 ml), 80°F (27°C)
- 2 tablespoons olive oil (30 ml)
- 1½ teaspoons salt (8.54 g)
- 3 cups bread flour (381 g)
- 1 tablespoon sugar (12.6 g)
- 1 cup Camembert cheese, rind removed and cubed (about 150 g)
- 1 medium apple, peeled, cored, and finely chopped (about 120 g)
- 1½ teaspoons active dry yeast (4.65 g)

 ## Instruction:

1. Prepare the Ingredients: Begin by adding the water and olive oil to the bread maker pan.
2. Add Dry Ingredients: Sprinkle in the salt and sugar. Then, add the bread flour. Create a small well in the center of the dry ingredients and add the yeast to this well.
3. Add Cheese and Apple: Distribute the cubed Camembert and finely chopped apple evenly over the flour. If your bread maker has a mix-in feature, add them at the signal; otherwise, include them at the beginning to ensure they're well incorporated into the dough.
4. Select the Cycle: Choose the Basic or White Bread setting on your bread maker.
5. Start the Bread Maker: Close the lid and start the machine. The bread maker will mix, knead, rise, and bake the Camembert and Apple Bread.
6. Cool Before Slicing: Once the baking cycle is complete, carefully remove the bread pan from the machine. Let the bread cool in the pan for about 5-10 minutes before turning it out onto a wire rack to cool completely.
7. Serve: Slice the bread and enjoy! The Camembert and Apple Bread offers a delightful combination of flavors, perfect for a sophisticated breakfast, a snack, or as part of a cheese board.

Pepperoni Bread

Prep: 10 Min

Serves: 1 loaf (12 slices)

Ingredient:

- 1 cup + 2 tablespoons water (270 ml), 80°F (27°C)
- 2 tablespoons olive oil (30 ml)
- 1½ teaspoons salt (8.54 g)
- 3 cups bread flour (381 g)
- 1 tablespoon sugar (12.6 g)
- 1 cup thinly sliced pepperoni (about 100 g), chop if slices are large.
- 1½ teaspoons active dry yeast (4.65 g)

Instruction:

1. Prepare the Ingredients: Begin by adding the water and olive oil to the bread maker pan.
2. Add Dry Ingredients: Sprinkle in the salt and sugar. Then, add the bread flour. Make a small well in the center of the dry ingredients and add the yeast to this well.
3. Add Pepperoni: Distribute the thinly sliced (or chopped) pepperoni evenly over the flour. If your bread maker has a mix-in feature, add the pepperoni at the signal; otherwise, include them at the beginning to ensure they're well incorporated into the dough.
4. Select the Cycle: Choose the Basic or White Bread setting on your bread maker.
5. Close the lid and start the machine. The bread maker will mix, knead, rise, and bake the Pepperoni Bread.
6. Once the baking cycle is complete, carefully remove the bread pan from the machine. Let the bread cool in the pan for about 5-10 minutes before turning it out onto a wire rack to cool completely.
7. Slice the bread and enjoy! Pepperoni Bread is perfect as a snack, for sandwiches, or as a side to your favorite Italian dishes.

CHAPTER 04: MEAT BREAD

Bacon Cheddar Bread

Prep: 15 Min

Serves: 1 loaf (12 slices)

Ingredient:

- 1 cup + 2 tablespoons water (270 ml), 80°F (27°C)
- 2 tablespoons olive oil (30 ml)
- 1½ teaspoons salt (8.54 g)
- 3 cups bread flour (381 g)
- 1 tablespoon sugar (12.6 g)
- ¾ cup cooked and crumbled bacon (about 6 slices or 90 g)
- 1 cup shredded sharp cheddar cheese (100 g)
- 1½ teaspoons active dry yeast (4.65 g)

Instruction:

1. Prepare the Bread Maker: Start by adding the water and olive oil to the bread maker pan.
2. Add Dry Ingredients: Sprinkle in the salt and sugar. Then, add the bread flour. Create a small well in the center of the dry ingredients and add the yeast to this well.
3. Add Bacon and Cheese: Evenly distribute the cooked, crumbled bacon and shredded sharp cheddar cheese over the flour. If your bread maker has a mix-in feature, add them at the beep signal; otherwise, add them at the beginning to ensure they're well incorporated.
4. Select the Cycle: Choose the Basic or White Bread setting on your bread maker.
5. Close the lid and start the machine. The bread maker will mix, knead, rise, and bake the Bacon Cheddar Bread.
6. Cool Before Slicing: After the baking cycle completes, carefully remove the bread pan from the machine. Let the bread cool in the pan for about 5-10 minutes before turning it out onto a wire rack to cool completely.
7. Serve: Slice the bread and enjoy! Bacon Cheddar Bread is delicious when served warm, offering a savory and cheesy flavor that's perfect for breakfast or as a side to any meal.

Sausage and Herb Bread

Prep: 15 Min

Serves: 1 loaf (12 slices)

Ingredient:

- 1 cup + 2 tablespoons water (270 ml), 80°F (27°C)
- 2 tablespoons olive oil (30 ml)
- 1½ teaspoons salt (8.54 g)
- 3 cups bread flour (381 g)
- 1 tablespoon sugar (12.6 g)
- ¾ cup cooked, crumbled sausage (about 100 g)
- 1 tablespoon mixed dried herbs (such as rosemary, thyme, and oregano) (3 g)
- 1½ teaspoons active dry yeast (4.65 g)

 ## Instruction:

1. Prepare the Sausage: Cook the sausage until fully browned, then crumble or chop into small pieces. Allow it to cool slightly before adding to the bread maker.
2. Add Liquids to Bread Maker Pan: Begin by pouring the water into the bread maker pan. Add the olive oil.
3. Add Dry Ingredients: Sprinkle in the salt and sugar. Then, add the bread flour. Make a small well in the center of the dry ingredients and add the yeast.
4. Add Sausage and Herbs: Evenly distribute the cooked, crumbled sausage and mixed dried herbs over the flour. If your bread maker has a mix-in feature, add them at the beep signal; otherwise, add them at the beginning to ensure they're well incorporated.
5. Choose the Basic or White Bread setting on your bread maker.
6. Close the lid and start the machine. The bread maker will mix, knead, rise, and bake the Sausage and Herb Bread.
7. Once the baking cycle is complete, carefully remove the bread pan from the machine. Let the bread cool in the pan for about 5-10 minutes before turning it out onto a wire rack to cool completely.
8. Slice the bread and enjoy! Sausage and Herb Bread is perfect as a savory breakfast option, a hearty side for soups and salads, or as the base for an unforgettable sandwich.

CHAPTER 04: MEAT BREAD

Ham and Swiss Bread

Prep: 10 Min

Serves: 1 loaf (12 slices)

Ingredient:

- 1 cup + 2 tablespoons water (270 ml), 80°F (27°C)
- 2 tablespoons olive oil (30 ml)
- 1½ teaspoons salt (8.54 g)
- 3 cups bread flour (381 g)
- 1 tablespoon sugar (12.6 g)
- ¾ cup finely chopped cooked ham (about 100 g)
- 1 cup shredded Swiss cheese (100 g)
- 1½ teaspoons active dry yeast (4.65 g)

 ## Instruction:

1. Prepare the Ingredients: Begin by adding the water and olive oil to the bread maker pan.
2. Add Dry Ingredients: Sprinkle in the salt and sugar. Then, add the bread flour. Create a small well in the center of the dry ingredients and add the yeast to this well.
3. Add Ham and Cheese: Evenly distribute the finely chopped cooked ham and shredded Swiss cheese over the flour. If your bread maker has a mix-in feature, use it to add the ham and cheese at the signal; otherwise, add them at the beginning to ensure they're well incorporated into the dough.
4. Select the Cycle: Choose the Basic or White Bread setting on your bread maker.
5. Close the lid and start the machine. The bread maker will mix, knead, rise, and bake the Ham and Swiss Bread.
6. Once the baking cycle is complete, carefully remove the bread pan from the machine. Let the bread cool in the pan for about 5-10 minutes before turning it out onto a wire rack to cool completely.
7. Slice the bread and enjoy! Ham and Swiss Bread is delicious when served warm, offering a savory and cheesy flavor that's perfect for breakfast, as a sandwich base, or as a side to your favorite meals.

Salami and Olive Bread

Prep: 10   Min

Serves: 1 loaf (12 slices)

Ingredient:

- 1 cup + 2 tablespoons water (270 ml), 80°F (27°C)
- 2 tablespoons olive oil (30 ml)
- 1½ teaspoons salt (8.54 g)
- 3 cups bread flour (381 g)
- 1 tablespoon sugar (12.6 g)
- ¾ cup chopped salami (about 100 g)
- ¾ cup chopped olives (green or black, or a mix; drained if using canned) (about 100 g)
- 1½ teaspoons active dry yeast (4.65 g)

Instruction:

1. Prepare the Ingredients: Start by adding the water and olive oil to the bread maker pan.
2. Add Dry Ingredients: Sprinkle the salt and sugar over the liquid. Then, add the bread flour. Create a small well in the center of the dry ingredients and add the yeast.
3. Add Salami and Olives: Evenly distribute the chopped salami and olives over the flour. If your bread maker has a mix-in feature, use it to add the salami and olives at the beep signal; otherwise, add them at the beginning to ensure they're well incorporated.
4. Select the Cycle: Choose the Basic or White Bread setting on your bread maker. This cycle is ideal for achieving a soft texture and fully integrating the savory ingredients.
5. Start the Bread Maker: Close the lid and start the machine. The bread maker will mix, knead, rise, and bake the Salami and Olive Bread.
6. Cool Before Slicing: Once the baking cycle is complete, carefully remove the bread pan from the machine. Let the bread cool in the pan for about 5-10 minutes before turning it out onto a wire rack to cool completely.
7. Serve: Slice the bread and enjoy! Salami and Olive Bread is perfect for sandwiches, as an appetizer, or as a hearty snack.

CHAPTER 04: MEAT BREAD

Italian Sausage and Parmesan Bread

Prep: 15   Min

Serves: 1 loaf (12 slices)

Ingredient:

- 1 cup + 2 tablespoons water (270 ml), 80°F (27°C)
- 2 tablespoons olive oil (30 ml)
- 1½ teaspoons salt (8.54 g)
- 3 cups bread flour (381 g)
- 1 tablespoon sugar (12.6 g)
- ¾ cup cooked and crumbled Italian sausage (about 100 g)
- 1 cup grated Parmesan cheese (100 g)
- 1½ teaspoons active dry yeast (4.65 g)

Instruction:

1. Prepare the Sausage: Cook the Italian sausage until fully browned, then crumble or chop into small pieces. Allow it to cool slightly before adding to the bread maker.
2. Add Liquids to Bread Maker Pan: Pour the water into the bread maker pan. Add the olive oil.
3. Add Dry Ingredients: Sprinkle the salt and sugar over the liquid. Then, add the bread flour. Create a small well in the center of the dry ingredients and add the yeast.
4. Add Sausage and Cheese: Evenly distribute the cooked, crumbled sausage and grated Parmesan cheese over the flour. If your bread maker has a mix-in feature, add them at the signal; otherwise, add them at the beginning to ensure they're well incorporated into the dough.
5. Select the Cycle: Choose the Basic or White Bread setting on your bread maker.
6. Close the lid and start the machine. The bread maker will mix, knead, rise, and bake the Italian Sausage and Parmesan Bread.
7. Once the baking cycle is complete, carefully remove the bread pan from the machine. Let the bread cool in the pan for about 5-10 minutes before turning it out onto a wire rack to cool completely.
8. Slice the bread and enjoy!

Chorizo and Cheese Bread

Prep: 15 Min

Serves: 1 loaf (12 slices)

Ingredient:

- 1 cup + 2 tablespoons water (270 ml), 80°F (27°C)
- 2 tablespoons olive oil (30 ml)
- 1½ teaspoons salt (8.54 g)
- 3 cups bread flour (381 g)
- 1 tablespoon sugar (12.6 g)
- 1 cup grated cheese (choose a type that complements chorizo, such as cheddar or pepper jack, about 100 g)
- ¾ cup cooked and crumbled chorizo (about 100 g)
- 1½ teaspoons active dry yeast (4.65 g)

 ## Instruction:

1. Prepare the Chorizo: If not pre-cooked, cook the chorizo in a pan until fully done, then let it cool and crumble or chop it into small pieces.
2. Add Liquids to Bread Maker Pan: Pour the water and olive oil into the bread maker pan.
3. Add Dry Ingredients: Add the salt, sugar, and bread flour to the pan. Make a small well in the center of the flour and add the yeast to this well.
4. Add Chorizo and Cheese: Distribute the cooked, crumbled chorizo and grated cheese evenly over the flour. If your bread maker has a mix-in feature and notifies you when to add mix-ins, use it; otherwise, add them at the beginning to ensure they're well incorporated into the dough.
5. Choose the Basic or White Bread setting on your bread maker.
6. Close the lid and start the cycle. The machine will take care of mixing, kneading, rising, and baking the Chorizo and Cheese Bread.
7. Once the baking cycle is complete, carefully remove the bread pan from the machine. Let the bread cool in the pan for about 10 minutes before transferring it to a wire rack to cool completely.
8. Serve: Slice the bread and enjoy it warm or at room temperature.

CHAPTER 04: MEAT BREAD

Beef and Onion Bread

Prep: 20 Min

Serves: 1 loaf (12 slices)

Ingredient:

- 1 cup + 2 tablespoons water (270 ml), 80°F (27°C)
- 2 tablespoons olive oil (30 ml)
- 1½ teaspoons salt (8.54 g)
- 3 cups bread flour (381 g)
- 1 tablespoon sugar (12.6 g)
- ¾ cup cooked, finely chopped beef (about 100 g) - use leftover roast beef or cooked ground beef for best results
- ½ cup caramelized onions (about 75 g) - lightly sauté onions until golden and sweet
- 1½ teaspoons active dry yeast (4.65 g)

 ## Instruction:

1. Prepare the Ingredients: Begin by adding the water and olive oil to the bread maker pan.
2. Add Dry Ingredients: Sprinkle in the salt and sugar. Then, add the bread flour. Create a small well in the center of the dry ingredients and add the yeast.
3. Add Beef and Onions: Evenly distribute the cooked, finely chopped beef and caramelized onions over the flour. If your bread maker has a mix-in feature, add them at the beep signal; otherwise, add them at the beginning to ensure they're well incorporated into the dough.
4. Select the Cycle: Choose the Basic or White Bread setting on your bread maker.
5. Start the Bread Maker: Close the lid and start the machine. The bread maker will mix, knead, rise, and bake the Beef and Onion Bread.
6. Cool Before Slicing: Once the baking cycle is complete, carefully remove the bread pan from the machine. Let the bread cool in the pan for about 5-10 minutes before turning it out onto a wire rack to cool completely.
7. Serve: Slice the bread and enjoy! Beef and Onion Bread is especially delicious when served warm, offering a rich and savory flavor that pairs well with a variety of dishes.

Chicken and Garlic Bread

Prep: 10   Min

Serves: 1 loaf (12 slices)

Ingredient:

- 1 cup + 2 tablespoons water (270 ml), 80°F (27°C)
- 2 tablespoons olive oil (30 ml)
- 1½ teaspoons salt (8.54 g)
- 3 cups bread flour (381 g)
- 1 tablespoon sugar (12.6 g)
- ¾ cup cooked, finely chopped chicken (about 100 g)
- 2 tablespoons finely minced garlic (about 6 g) or to taste
- 1½ teaspoons active dry yeast (4.65 g)

Instruction:

1. Prepare the Ingredients: Start by adding the water and olive oil to the bread maker pan.
2. Add Dry Ingredients: Sprinkle the salt and sugar into the pan. Then, add the bread flour. Make a small well in the center of the dry ingredients and add the yeast to this well.
3. Add Chicken and Garlic: Evenly distribute the cooked, finely chopped chicken and minced garlic over the flour. If your bread maker has a mix-in feature, add them at the beep signal; otherwise, include them at the beginning to ensure they're well incorporated into the dough.
4. Select the Cycle: Choose the Basic or White Bread setting on your bread maker.
5. Start the Bread Maker: Close the lid and start the machine. The bread maker will mix, knead, rise, and bake the Chicken and Garlic Bread.
6. Cool Before Slicing: Once the baking cycle is complete, carefully remove the bread pan from the machine. Let the bread cool in the pan for about 5-10 minutes before turning it out onto a wire rack to cool completely.
7. Serve: Slice the bread and enjoy! Chicken and Garlic Bread is especially delicious when served warm, making it a perfect accompaniment to meals or as a satisfying snack on its own.

CHAPTER 04: MEAT BREAD

Turkey and Cranberry Bread

Prep: 10   Min

Serves: 1 loaf (12 slices)

Ingredient:

- 1 cup + 2 tablespoons water (270 ml), 80°F (27°C)
- 2 tablespoons olive oil (30 ml)
- 1½ teaspoons salt (8.54 g)
- 3 cups bread flour (381 g)
- 1 tablespoon sugar (12.6 g)
- ¾ cup cooked turkey, finely chopped (about 100 g)
- ¾ cup dried cranberries (about 90 g)
- 1½ teaspoons active dry yeast (4.65 g)

Instruction:

1. Add Liquids to Bread Maker Pan: Begin by pouring the water into the bread maker pan. Add the olive oil.
2. Add Dry Ingredients: Sprinkle in the salt and sugar. Then, add the bread flour. Create a small well in the center of the dry ingredients and add the yeast to this well.
3. Add Turkey and Cranberries: Evenly distribute the finely chopped cooked turkey and dried cranberries over the flour. If your bread maker has a mix-in feature, add them at the signal; otherwise, add them at the beginning to ensure they're well incorporated into the dough.
4. Select the Cycle: Choose the Basic or White Bread setting on your bread maker. This cycle is ideal for achieving a soft texture and fully integrating the savory turkey and sweet cranberries.
5. Close the lid and start the machine. The bread maker will mix, knead, rise, and bake the Turkey and Cranberry Bread.
6. Once the baking cycle is complete, carefully remove the bread pan from the machine. Let the bread cool in the pan for about 5-10 minutes before turning it out onto a wire rack to cool completely.
7. Slice the bread and enjoy! This Turkey and Cranberry Bread is perfect for post-holiday meals, as a delightful breakfast option, or as a unique sandwich base.

Prosciutto and Mozzarella Bread

Prep: 10 Min

Serves: 1 loaf (12 slices)

Ingredient:

- 1 cup + 2 tablespoons water (270 ml), 80°F (27°C)
- 2 tablespoons olive oil (30 ml)
- 1½ teaspoons salt (8.54 g)
- 3 cups bread flour (381 g)
- 1 tablespoon sugar (12.6 g)
- ¾ cup diced prosciutto (about 100 g)
- 1 cup shredded mozzarella cheese (100 g)
- 1½ teaspoons active dry yeast (4.65 g)

 ## Instruction:

1. Prepare the Ingredients: Begin by adding the water and olive oil to the bread maker pan.
2. Add Dry Ingredients: Sprinkle in the salt and sugar. Then, add the bread flour. Make a small well in the center of the dry ingredients and add the yeast.
3. Add Prosciutto and Cheese: Evenly distribute the diced prosciutto and shredded mozzarella cheese over the flour. If your bread maker has a mix-in feature, add them at the signal; otherwise, add them at the beginning to ensure they're well incorporated into the dough.
4. Select the Cycle: Choose the Basic or White Bread setting on your bread maker.
5. Start the Bread Maker: Close the lid and start the machine. The bread maker will mix, knead, rise, and bake the Prosciutto and Mozzarella Bread.
6. Cool Before Slicing: Once the baking cycle is complete, carefully remove the bread pan from the machine. Let the bread cool in the pan for about 5-10 minutes before turning it out onto a wire rack to cool completely.
7. Slice the bread and enjoy! Prosciutto and Mozzarella Bread is perfect for sandwiches, as an accompaniment to Italian dishes, or enjoyed on its own to savor the flavors.

CHAPTER 04: MEAT BREAD

Ground Beef and Jalapeño Bread

Prep: 15 Min

Serves: 1 loaf (12 slices)

Ingredient:

- 1 cup + 2 tablespoons water (270 ml), 80°F (27°C)
- 2 tablespoons olive oil (30 ml)
- 1½ teaspoons salt (8.54 g)
- 3 cups bread flour (381 g)
- 1 tablespoon sugar (12.6 g)
- ¾ cup cooked ground beef, drained (about 100 g)
- 2 to 3 jalapeños, finely chopped (adjust based on heat preference), seeds removed for less heat (about 30 to 45 g)
- 1½ teaspoons active dry yeast (4.65 g)

 ## Instruction:

1. Prepare the Ground Beef: Cook the ground beef until fully browned, then drain any excess fat. Let it cool slightly before adding to the bread maker.
2. Add Liquids to Bread Maker Pan: Start by pouring the water into the bread maker pan. Add the olive oil.
3. Add Dry Ingredients: Sprinkle in the salt and sugar. Then, add the bread flour. Make a small well in the center of the dry ingredients and add the yeast.
4. Add Beef and Jalapeños: Evenly distribute the cooked ground beef and finely chopped jalapeños over the flour. If your bread maker has a mix-in feature, add them at the signal; otherwise, add them at the beginning to ensure they're well incorporated into the dough.
5. Choose the Basic or White Bread setting on your bread maker.
6. Close the lid and start the machine. The bread maker will mix, knead, rise, and bake the Ground Beef and Jalapeño Bread.
7. Once the baking cycle is complete, carefully remove the bread pan from the machine. Let the bread cool in the pan for about 5-10 minutes before turning it out onto a wire rack to cool completely.
8. Serve: Slice the bread and enjoy!

Corned Beef and Caraway Seed Bread

Prep: 10 Min

Serves: 1 loaf (12 slices)

Ingredient:

- 1 cup + 2 tablespoons water (270 ml), 80°F (27°C)
- 2 tablespoons olive oil (30 ml)
- 3 cups bread flour (381 g)
- 1½ teaspoons salt (8.54 g)
- 1 tablespoon sugar (12.6 g)
- 1 cup finely chopped corned beef (about 150 g)
- 2 tablespoons caraway seeds (about 18 g)
- 1½ teaspoons active dry yeast (4.65 g)

 ## Instruction:

1. Prepare the Ingredients: Start by chopping the corned beef into small, fine pieces to ensure even distribution throughout the bread.
2. Add Liquids to Bread Maker Pan: Pour the water and olive oil into the bread maker pan.
3. Add Dry Ingredients: Over the liquids, add the bread flour, salt, and sugar. Make a small well in the center of the dry ingredients and add the yeast to this well.
4. Add Corned Beef and Caraway Seeds: Evenly distribute the chopped corned beef and caraway seeds over the flour. If your bread maker has an add-in feature, follow the machine's prompts for adding these ingredients; otherwise, they can be added at the beginning.
5. Set your bread maker to the Basic or White Bread setting.
6. Close the lid and start the cycle. The machine will take care of the rest, ensuring the ingredients are thoroughly combined and the bread is baked to perfection.
7. Once the baking cycle is complete, carefully remove the bread pan from the machine. Let the bread cool in the pan for about 10 minutes before transferring it to a wire rack to cool completely.
8. Slice the Corned Beef and Caraway Seed Bread and enjoy.

CHAPTER 04: MEAT BREAD

Pulled Pork and BBQ Sauce Bread

Prep: 10 Min

Serves: 1 loaf (12 slices)

Ingredient:

- 1 cup water (240 ml), 80°F (27°C)
- ¼ cup BBQ sauce (60 ml)
- 2 tablespoons olive oil (30 ml)
- 3 cups bread flour (381 g)
- 1 tablespoon sugar (12.6 g)
- 1½ teaspoons salt (8.54 g)
- 1 cup cooked, shredded pulled pork (about 150 g)
- 1½ teaspoons active dry yeast (4.65 g)

 ## Instruction:

1. Prepare the Ingredients: Ensure the pulled pork is finely shredded and mixed with a bit of BBQ sauce to enhance its flavor without making it too wet.
2. Mix Liquids: In the bread maker pan, combine the water, BBQ sauce, and olive oil.
3. Add Dry Ingredients: Over the liquids, evenly add the bread flour, sugar, and salt. Make a small well in the center of the flour and add the yeast to this well.
4. Add Pulled Pork: Evenly distribute the shredded pulled pork over the flour. If your bread maker has an add-in feature, use it according to the manufacturer's instructions; otherwise, add the pork at the beginning to ensure it's well incorporated into the dough.
5. Choose the Basic or White Bread setting on your bread maker.
6. Close the lid and start the cycle. The machine will take care of mixing the ingredients, kneading the dough, letting it rise, and baking it to perfection.
7. Once the cycle is complete, carefully remove the bread pan from the machine, and let the bread cool in the pan for about 10 minutes before transferring it to a wire rack to cool completely.
8. Slice the Pulled Pork and BBQ Sauce Bread and enjoy. This bread is excellent when served warm, making it a perfect match for additional BBQ sauce, butter, or as the base for an innovative sandwich.

Lamb and Rosemary Bread

Prep: 15   Min

Serves: 1 loaf (12 slices)

Ingredient:

- 1 cup + 2 tablespoons water (270 ml), 80°F (27°C)
- 2 tablespoons olive oil (30 ml)
- 1½ teaspoons salt (8.54 g)
- 3 cups bread flour (381 g)
- 1 tablespoon sugar (12.6 g)
- ¾ cup cooked, finely chopped lamb (about 100 g)
- 2 tablespoons fresh rosemary, chopped (or 2 teaspoons dried rosemary) (6 g if fresh, 2 g if dried)
- 1½ teaspoons active dry yeast (4.65 g)

Instruction:

1. Prepare the Lamb: Cook the lamb until fully cooked, then finely chop. Allow it to cool slightly before adding to the bread maker.
2. Add Liquids to Bread Maker Pan: Begin by pouring the water into the bread maker pan. Add the olive oil.
3. Add Dry Ingredients: Sprinkle in the salt and sugar. Then, add the bread flour. Make a small well in the center of the dry ingredients and add the yeast.
4. Add Lamb and Rosemary: Evenly distribute the cooked, chopped lamb and rosemary over the flour. If your bread maker has a mix-in feature, add them at the signal; otherwise, add them at the beginning to ensure they're well incorporated.
5. Choose the Basic or White Bread setting on your bread maker.
6. Close the lid and start the machine. The bread maker will mix, knead, rise, and bake the Lamb and Rosemary Bread.
7. Once the baking cycle is complete, carefully remove the bread pan from the machine. Let the bread cool in the pan for about 5-10 minutes before turning it out onto a wire rack to cool completely.
8. Slice the bread and enjoy! Lamb and Rosemary Bread is delicious when served warm, offering a unique combination of flavors that's perfect for a special occasion or to elevate your daily meals.

CHAPTER 04: MEAT BREAD

Duck and Orange Zest Bread

Prep: 20   Min

Serves: 1 loaf (12 slices)

Ingredient:

- 1 cup + 2 tablespoons water (270 ml), 80°F (27°C)
- 2 tablespoons olive oil (30 ml)
- 1½ teaspoons salt (8.54 g)
- 3 cups bread flour (381 g)
- 1 tablespoon sugar (12.6 g)
- ¾ cup cooked, finely shredded duck meat (about 100 g)
- Zest of 1 large orange (about 2 tablespoons or 6 g)
- 1½ teaspoons active dry yeast (4.65 g)

Instruction:

1. Prepare Duck and Orange Zest: Cook the duck (roasting or simmering works well) until tender, then finely shred the meat. Zest one large orange, being careful to avoid the bitter white pith.
2. Add Liquids to Bread Maker Pan: Pour the water into the bread maker pan. Add the olive oil.
3. Add Dry Ingredients: Sprinkle in the salt and sugar. Then, add the bread flour. Make a small well in the center of the dry ingredients and add the yeast.
4. Add Duck and Orange Zest: Evenly distribute the shredded duck and orange zest over the flour. If your bread maker has a mix-in feature, add them at the signal; otherwise, add them at the beginning to ensure they're well incorporated into the dough.
5. Select the Cycle: Choose the Basic or White Bread setting on your bread maker.
6. Start the Bread Maker: Close the lid and start the machine. The bread maker will mix, knead, rise, and bake the Duck and Orange Zest Bread.
7. Cool Before Slicing: Once the baking cycle is complete, carefully remove the bread pan from the machine. Let the bread cool in the pan for about 5-10 minutes before turning it out onto a wire rack to cool completely.
8. Serve: Slice the bread and enjoy!

Venison and Berry Bread

Prep: 20 Min

Serves: 1 loaf (12 slices)

Ingredient:

- 1 cup + 2 tablespoons water (270 ml), 80°F (27°C)
- 2 tablespoons olive oil (30 ml)
- 1½ teaspoons salt (8.54 g)
- 3 cups bread flour (381 g)
- 1 tablespoon sugar (12.6 g)
- ¾ cup cooked, finely ground or shredded venison (about 100 g)
- ¾ cup mixed berries (fresh or if using frozen, ensure they are thawed and well-drained) (about 100 g)
- 1½ teaspoons active dry yeast (4.65 g)

Instruction:

1. Prepare Venison and Berries: Cook the venison until fully done, then finely grind or shred it. Prepare the berries by ensuring they are clean and, if frozen, thawed and thoroughly drained to remove excess moisture.
2. Add Liquids to Bread Maker Pan: Start by pouring the water into the bread maker pan. Add the olive oil.
3. Add Dry Ingredients: Sprinkle in the salt and sugar. Then, add the bread flour. Create a small well in the center of the dry ingredients and add the yeast.
4. Add Venison and Berries: Evenly distribute the venison and berries over the flour. If your bread maker has a mix-in feature, add them at the signal; otherwise, add them at the beginning to ensure they're well incorporated into the dough.
5. Choose the Basic or White Bread setting on your bread maker.
6. Close the lid and start the machine. The bread maker will mix, knead, rise, and bake the Venison and Berry Bread.
7. Once the baking cycle is complete, carefully remove the bread pan from the machine. Let the bread cool in the pan for about 5-10 minutes before turning it out onto a wire rack to cool completely.
8. Slice the bread and enjoy!

CHAPTER 04: MEAT BREAD

Pork Belly and Apple Bread

Prep: 15 Min

Serves: 1 loaf (12 slices)

Ingredient:

- 1 cup + 2 tablespoons lukewarm water (270 ml), 80°F (27°C)
- 2 tablespoons olive oil (30 ml)
- 3 cups bread flour (381 g)
- 1 tablespoon sugar (12.6 g)
- 1½ teaspoons salt (8.54 g)
- 1 cup cooked pork belly, finely chopped (about 150 g)
- 1 cup apple, peeled and finely diced (about 115 g)
- 1 teaspoon cinnamon (optional for a hint of warmth) (2.6 g)
- 1½ teaspoons active dry yeast (4.65 g)

Instruction:

1. Cook Pork Belly: Ensure the pork belly is cooked thoroughly and chopped into small pieces. Let it cool before adding it to the bread maker.
2. Prepare Apples: Peel and finely dice the apple. To prevent browning, you can toss the diced apple in a little lemon juice.
3. Add Wet Ingredients: Pour the lukewarm water and olive oil into the bread maker pan.
4. Add Dry Ingredients: Over the wet ingredients, evenly spread the bread flour, sugar, and salt. If using, sprinkle the cinnamon over the flour.
5. Make a Well for Yeast: Create a small well in the center of the dry ingredients (not too deep) and add the yeast to this well.
6. Add Pork Belly and Apple: Distribute the finely chopped pork belly and diced apple over the flour. If your bread maker has a mix-in feature, follow the machine's prompts; otherwise, add them at the beginning.
7. Select the Cycle: Set your bread maker to the Basic or White Bread Cycle.
8. Close the lid and start the selected cycle.
9. Once the baking cycle is complete, carefully remove the bread pan from the machine, and let the bread cool in the pan for about 10 minutes before transferring it to a wire rack to cool completely.
10. Slice the Pork Belly and Apple Bread and enjoy.

Meatball Marinara Bread

Prep: 15 Min

Serves: 1 loaf (12 slices)

Ingredient:

- 1 cup + 2 tablespoons water (270 ml), 80°F (27°C)
- 2 tablespoons olive oil (30 ml)
- 1½ teaspoons salt (8.54 g)
- 3 cups bread flour (381 g)
- 1 tablespoon sugar (12.6 g)
- ¾ cup cooked meatballs, finely chopped (about 100 g)
- ½ cup marinara sauce (reduce liquid as much as possible to concentrate flavors) (about 120 ml, reduced)
- 1 tablespoon Italian seasoning (3 g)
- 1½ teaspoons active dry yeast (4.65 g)

Instruction:

1. Ensure meatballs are fully cooked and finely chopped. If your marinara sauce is very liquidy, consider reducing it on the stove to concentrate the flavors and minimize added moisture. Let both components cool to room temperature before adding.
2. Begin by pouring the water and olive oil into the bread maker pan. Add the reduced marinara sauce.
3. Sprinkle in the salt and sugar. Then, add the bread flour. Sprinkle the Italian seasoning over the flour. Make a small well in the center of the dry ingredients and add the yeast.
4. Add Meatballs: Evenly distribute the finely chopped meatballs over the flour. If your bread maker has a mix-in feature, add them at the signal; otherwise, add them at the beginning to ensure they're well incorporated.
5. Choose the Basic or White Bread setting on your bread maker.
6. Close the lid and start the machine. The bread maker will mix, knead, rise, and bake the Meatball Marinara Bread.
7. Once the baking cycle is complete, carefully remove the bread pan from the machine. Let the bread cool in the pan for about 5-10 minutes before turning it out onto a wire rack to cool completely.
8. Serve: Slice the bread and enjoy!

CHAPTER 04: MEAT BREAD

Bacon and Maple Syrup Bread

Prep: 15 Min

Serves: 1 loaf (12 slices)

Ingredient:

- 1 cup + 2 tablespoons water (270 ml), 80°F (27°C)
- 2 tablespoons olive oil (30 ml)
- 1½ teaspoons salt (8.54 g)
- 3 cups bread flour (381 g)
- 1 tablespoon sugar (12.6 g)
- ¾ cup cooked and crumbled bacon (about 100 g)
- ¼ cup pure maple syrup (60 ml)
- 1½ teaspoons active dry yeast (4.65 g)

Instruction:

1. Cook the bacon until crispy, then crumble or chop into small pieces. Let it cool to room temperature before adding to the bread maker.
2. Start by pouring the water into the bread maker pan. Add the olive oil and maple syrup.
3. Sprinkle in the salt and sugar. Then, add the bread flour. Create a small well in the center of the dry ingredients and add the yeast.
4. Evenly distribute the cooked, crumbled bacon over the flour. If your bread maker has a mix-in feature, add the bacon at the signal; otherwise, add it at the beginning to ensure it's well incorporated.
5. Choose the Basic or White Bread setting on your bread maker.
6. Close the lid and start the machine. The bread maker will mix, knead, rise, and bake the Bacon and Maple Syrup Bread.
7. Once the baking cycle is complete, carefully remove the bread pan from the machine. Let the bread cool in the pan for about 5-10 minutes before turning it out onto a wire rack to cool completely.
8. Slice the bread and enjoy! Bacon and Maple Syrup Bread is perfect for breakfast, offering a delicious balance of savory and sweet flavors. Enjoy it as is, toast it for a crispy treat, or use it to create unique sandwiches.

Cinnamon Raisin Bread

Prep: 5 Min

Serves: 1 loaf (12 slices)

Ingredient:

- 1 cup water (240 ml), 80°F (27°C)
- 2 tablespoons butter, softened (30 ml)
- 3 cups bread flour (381 g)
- ¼ cup sugar (50 g)
- 1½ teaspoons salt (8.54 g)
- 2 teaspoons ground cinnamon (5.2 g)
- 2 teaspoons active dry yeast (6.4 g)
- ¾ cup raisins (120 g)

Instruction:

1. Add Liquids to Bread Maker Pan: Begin by adding the water and softened butter into the bread maker pan.
2. Add Dry Ingredients: Next, add the bread flour, ensuring it covers the liquid. Sprinkle the sugar, salt, and ground cinnamon evenly over the flour. Make a small well in the center of the dry ingredients (not too deep) and carefully add the yeast to this well.
3. Add Raisins: If your bread maker has an add-in feature for nuts or fruits, add the raisins when the machine prompts you. Otherwise, you can add the raisins at the beginning to ensure they're evenly distributed throughout the dough, or wait until the final kneading cycle begins to add them.
4. Choose the Sweet Bread Cycle on your bread maker.
5. Close the lid and start the selected cycle. The machine will handle the mixing, kneading, rising, and baking processes.
6. Once the cycle is complete and the bread is baked, carefully remove the bread pan from the machine. Let the bread cool in the pan for about 10 minutes before transferring it to a wire rack to cool completely.
7. Slice the Cinnamon Raisin Bread and enjoy it warm or at room temperature. It's delicious on its own, toasted with butter, or as the base for French toast.

CHAPTER 05: SWEET BREAD

Chocolate Chip Bread

Prep: 5 Min

Serves: 1 loaf (12 slices)

Ingredient:

- 1 cup + 2 tablespoons water (270 ml), 80°F (27°C)
- 2 tablespoons olive oil (30 ml)
- 1½ teaspoons salt (8.54 g)
- 3 cups bread flour (381 g)
- 2 tablespoons sugar (25.2 g) - Adjusted for sweetness
- ¾ cup semi-sweet chocolate chips (about 130 g)
- 1½ teaspoons active dry yeast (4.65 g)

Instruction:

1. Prepare the Bread Maker: Pour the water and olive oil into the bread maker pan.
2. Add Dry Ingredients: Add the salt, sugar, and bread flour to the pan. Make a small well in the center of the flour (not too deep) and add the yeast to this well.
3. Add Chocolate Chips: Distribute the chocolate chips evenly over the flour. If your bread maker has an add-in feature and notifies you when to add mix-ins, use it; otherwise, add the chocolate chips at the beginning to ensure they're well incorporated.
4. Select the Cycle: Set your bread maker to the Sweet Bread Cycle.
5. Start the Bread Maker: Close the lid and start the selected cycle. The machine will handle the mixing, kneading, rising, and baking.
6. Cool Before Slicing: After the cycle completes, carefully remove the bread pan from the machine. Let the bread cool in the pan for about 10 minutes before transferring it to a wire rack to cool completely.

Banana Bread

Prep: 10 Min

Serves: 1 loaf (12 slices)

Ingredient:

- 3 ripe bananas, mashed (about 1 cup or 225 ml)
- 2 tablespoons olive oil (30 ml)
- 2 eggs, lightly beaten
- 1/3 cup milk (80 ml)
- 2 cups all-purpose flour (240 g)
- 3/4 cup sugar (150 g)
- 1 teaspoon baking powder (5 g)
- 1/2 teaspoon baking soda (2.5 g)
- 1/2 teaspoon salt (2.5 g)
- 1 teaspoon vanilla extract (5 ml)
- 1/2 cup chopped walnuts or pecans (optional) (60 g)

Instruction:

1. Prepare Wet Ingredients: In a medium bowl, mix together the mashed bananas, olive oil, eggs, milk, and vanilla extract until well combined.
2. Add Ingredients to Bread Maker Pan: Pour the wet mixture into the bread maker pan.
3. Mix Dry Ingredients: In another bowl, whisk together the flour, sugar, baking powder, baking soda, and salt. Gently pour this dry mixture over the wet ingredients in the bread maker pan. If adding nuts, sprinkle them on top of the dry ingredients.
4. Select the Cycle: Choose the Quick Bread or Cake setting on your bread maker.
5. Start the Bread Maker: Close the lid and start the selected cycle. The machine will mix and bake the banana bread.
6. Cool Before Slicing: Once the cycle is complete, carefully remove the bread pan from the machine. Let the banana bread cool in the pan for about 10 minutes before transferring it to a wire rack to cool completely.
7. Serve: Slice the banana bread and enjoy. It's delicious as is or served with butter, cream cheese, or a drizzle of honey.

CHAPTER 05: SWEET BREAD

Apple Cinnamon Bread

Prep: 10 Min

Serves: 1 loaf (12 slices)

Ingredient:

- 1 cup + 2 tablespoons water (270 ml), 80°F (27°C)
- 2 tablespoons olive oil (30 ml)
- 1½ teaspoons salt (8.54 g)
- 3 cups bread flour (381 g)
- ¼ cup sugar (50 g)
- 2 teaspoons ground cinnamon (5.2 g)
- 1 cup finely chopped or grated apple (about 1 large apple, 115 g)
- ½ cup raisins (optional) (80 g)
- 1½ teaspoons active dry yeast (4.65 g)

Instruction:

1. Prepare the Ingredients: Start by peeling (if preferred) and finely chopping or grating the apple. Measure the ingredients as listed.
2. Add Liquids to Bread Maker Pan: Pour the water and olive oil into the bread maker pan.
3. Add Dry Ingredients: Add the salt, sugar, bread flour, and ground cinnamon to the pan. Sprinkle the active dry yeast into a small well in the center of the flour.
4. Add Apples (and Raisins): Evenly distribute the chopped or grated apple (and raisins, if using) over the flour. If your bread maker has an add-in feature and notifies you when to add mix-ins, use it; otherwise, add the apples and raisins at the beginning to ensure they're well incorporated.
5. Select the Cycle: Set your bread maker to the Sweet Bread Cycle.
6. Close the lid and start the selected cycle. The bread maker will mix, knead, rise, and bake the Apple Cinnamon Bread.
7. Once the cycle is complete, carefully remove the bread pan from the machine. Allow the bread to cool in the pan for about 10 minutes before transferring it to a wire rack to cool completely.
8. Slice the bread and enjoy it warm or at room temperature. Apple Cinnamon Bread is delicious on its own, toasted with butter, or as a base for French toast for a special breakfast.

Pumpkin Spice Bread

Prep: 10   Min

Serves: 1 loaf (8 to 10 slices)

Ingredient:

- 1 cup canned pumpkin puree (245 ml)
- ¼ cup water (60 ml), 80°F (27°C)
- ¼ cup vegetable oil (60 ml)
- 2 eggs, lightly beaten
- 2 cups all-purpose flour (256 g)
- 1 cup sugar (200 g)
- 1½ teaspoons baking powder (7.5 g)
- ½ teaspoon baking soda (2.5 g)
- 1½ teaspoons salt (8.54 g)
- 2 teaspoons ground cinnamon (5.2 g)
- ½ teaspoon ground nutmeg (1.2 g)
- ½ teaspoon ground ginger (1.2 g)
- ¼ teaspoon ground cloves (0.6 g)
- 1½ teaspoons active dry yeast (4.65 g)

Instruction:

1. Combine Wet Ingredients: In a mixing bowl, combine the pumpkin puree, water, vegetable oil, and eggs. Stir until well blended.
2. Layer Ingredients in Bread Maker: Pour the wet mixture into the bread maker pan first. Then, evenly add the flour on top of the wet ingredients.
3. Add Remaining Dry Ingredients: Sprinkle the sugar, baking powder, baking soda, salt, cinnamon, nutmeg, ginger, and cloves over the flour. If using yeast (for bread makers that mix the batter), make a small well in the center of the dry ingredients and add the yeast.
4. Set your bread maker to the Sweet Bread or Cake Cycle.
5. Close the lid and start the cycle. The machine will mix the ingredients, then bake the Pumpkin Spice Bread.
6. After the cycle completes, carefully remove the bread pan from the machine. Let the bread cool in the pan for about 10 minutes before transferring it to a wire rack to cool completely.
7. Slice the Pumpkin Spice Bread and enjoy it warm or at room temperature. It's perfect as is, or you can enhance it with a spread of cream cheese or butter.

CHAPTER 05: SWEET BREAD

Blueberry Lemon Bread

Prep: 10   Min

Serves: 1 loaf (8 to 10 slices)

Ingredient:

- ¾ cup milk (180 ml), 80°F (27°C)
- ¼ cup melted butter (60 ml)
- 2 large eggs
- 1 teaspoon vanilla extract (5 ml)
- 3 cups all-purpose flour (381 g)
- 1 cup sugar (200 g)
- 1½ teaspoons baking powder (7.5 g)
- ½ teaspoon salt (2.5 g)
- Zest of 1 large lemon (about 1 tablespoon or 6 g)
- 1 cup fresh blueberries (if using frozen, do not thaw) (about 150 g)
- 1½ teaspoons active dry yeast (4.65 g)

Instruction:

1. Prepare Wet Ingredients: In a bowl, whisk together the milk, melted butter, eggs, and vanilla extract until well combined.
2. Layer Ingredients in Bread Maker Pan: Pour the wet mixture into the bread maker pan. Then, gently add the flour, covering the liquid.
3. Add Remaining Dry Ingredients: Sprinkle the sugar, baking powder, salt, and lemon zest over the flour. If your recipe requires yeast, make a small well in the center of the dry ingredients and add the yeast.
4. Carefully distribute the blueberries on top. If your bread maker has a mix-in beep, add the blueberries then; otherwise, add them with the other ingredients, but try to keep them towards the top to prevent them from getting crushed during the mixing phase.
5. Choose the Sweet Bread or Cake Cycle on your bread maker.
6. Close the lid and start the selected cycle. The machine will mix, knead (minimally, if at all, to avoid crushing the blueberries), and bake the Blueberry Lemon Bread.
7. Once the cycle is complete, carefully remove the bread pan from the machine. Allow the bread to cool in the pan for about 10 minutes before transferring it to a wire rack to cool completely.
8. Slice the Blueberry Lemon Bread and enjoy it warm or at room temperature.

Cranberry Orange Bread

Prep: 10 Min

Serves: 1 loaf (12 slices)

Ingredient:

- ¾ cup orange juice (180 ml), at room temperature (about 27°C)
- ¼ cup water (60 ml), at room temperature (about 27°C)
- 2 tablespoons olive oil (30 ml)
- 3 cups bread flour (381 g)
- ¼ cup sugar (50 g)
- 1½ teaspoons salt (8.54 g)
- Zest of 1 large orange (to yield approximately 2 tablespoons or 6 g)
- ¾ cup dried cranberries (90 g)
- 1½ teaspoons active dry yeast (4.65 g)

Instruction:

1. Combine Wet Ingredients: In the bread maker pan, combine the orange juice, water, and olive oil.
2. Add Dry Ingredients: Over the wet mixture, evenly add the bread flour. Then, sprinkle the sugar, salt, and orange zest across the flour. Create a small well in the center of the dry ingredients (not too deep) and carefully add the yeast to the well. This helps ensure the yeast doesn't activate too early.
3. Incorporate Cranberries: Evenly distribute the dried cranberries on top of the flour. If your bread maker includes a feature for adding nuts or fruits, follow the manufacturer's instructions; otherwise, they can be added before starting the cycle to mix throughout the dough.
4. Set your bread maker to the Sweet Bread Cycle.
5. Start the Bread Maker: Close the lid and start the cycle. The machine will take care of kneading, rising, and baking the Cranberry Orange Bread.
6. Once the baking cycle is complete, remove the bread pan from the machine using oven mitts. Allow the bread to cool in the pan for about 10 minutes before transferring it to a wire rack to cool completely.
7. Slice the cooled Cranberry Orange Bread and enjoy it either plain or with a spread of butter.

CHAPTER 05: SWEET BREAD

Pear and Ginger Bread

Prep: 10 Min

Serves: 1 loaf (12 slices)

Ingredient:

- ¾ cup pear juice (180 ml), 80°F (27°C)
- ¼ cup water (60 ml), 80°F (27°C)
- 2 tablespoons unsalted butter, melted (30 ml)
- 3 cups bread flour (381 g)
- ¼ cup sugar (50 g)
- 1½ teaspoons ground ginger (3 g)
- ½ teaspoon salt (2.5 g)
- 1 cup ripe pear, peeled and finely diced (about 1 large pear, 150 g)
- ¼ cup crystallized ginger, finely chopped (40 g)
- 1½ teaspoons active dry yeast (4.65 g)

Instruction:

1. Prepare Ingredients: Start by peeling and finely dicing the pear. Chop the crystallized ginger into small pieces.
2. Add Liquids to Bread Maker Pan: Pour the pear juice, water, and melted butter into the bread maker pan.
3. Add Dry Ingredients: Over the liquids, evenly add the bread flour. Then, sprinkle the sugar, ground ginger, and salt across the flour.
4. Add Pear and Ginger: Distribute the diced pear and crystallized ginger over the flour. If your bread maker has an add-in feature and notifies you when to add mix-ins, use it; otherwise, add them at the beginning to ensure they're well incorporated.
5. Add Yeast: Make a small well in the center of the dry ingredients (not too deep) and add the yeast to this well.
6. Choose the Sweet Bread Cycle on your bread maker.
7. Close the lid and start the cycle. The machine will take care of the mixing, kneading, rising, and baking processes.
8. Once the cycle is complete, carefully remove the bread pan from the machine, and let the bread cool in the pan for about 10 minutes before transferring it to a wire rack to cool completely.
9. Slice the Pear and Ginger Bread and enjoy it either warm or at room temperature. It pairs beautifully with a cup of tea or coffee.

Sweet Coconut Bread

Prep: 5   Min

Serves: 1 loaf (12 slices)

Ingredient:

- 1 cup coconut milk (240 ml), at room temperature
- ¼ cup water (60 ml), at room temperature
- 2 tablespoons melted coconut oil (30 ml)
- 3 cups bread flour (381 g)
- ½ cup sugar (100 g)
- ½ teaspoon salt (2.5 g)
- ¾ cup shredded coconut (60 g)
- 1½ teaspoons active dry yeast (4.65 g)

➤ Instruction:

1. Combine Liquids: In the bread maker pan, mix together the coconut milk, water, and melted coconut oil.
2. Add Dry Ingredients: Over the liquids, evenly add the bread flour. Then, sprinkle the sugar and salt across the flour.
3. Add Coconut and Yeast: Distribute the shredded coconut over the other ingredients. Make a small well in the center of the dry ingredients (not too deep) and carefully add the yeast to the well, ensuring it does not come into direct contact with the liquids yet.
4. Select the Cycle: Set your bread maker to the Sweet Bread Cycle.
5. Start the Bread Maker: Close the lid and start the cycle. The machine will take care of kneading, rising, and baking the Sweet Coconut Bread.
6. Cool Before Slicing: Once the cycle is complete, carefully remove the bread pan from the machine, and allow the bread to cool in the pan for about 10 minutes before transferring it to a wire rack to cool completely.
7. Serve: Slice the cooled Sweet Coconut Bread and enjoy it either plain, toasted, or with a spread of butter or jam for an extra treat.

CHAPTER 05: SWEET BREAD

Maple Pecan Bread

Prep: 5   Min

Serves: 1 loaf (12 slices)

Ingredient:

- ¾ cup milk (180 ml), at room temperature
- ¼ cup pure maple syrup (60 ml)
- 2 tablespoons unsalted butter, melted (30 ml)
- 3 cups bread flour (381 g)
- ¼ cup brown sugar (50 g)
- 1½ teaspoons salt (8.54 g)
- 1 cup chopped pecans (100 g)
- 1½ teaspoons active dry yeast (4.65 g)

➤ Instruction:

1. Combine Liquids: In the bread maker pan, combine the milk, maple syrup, and melted butter.
2. Add Dry Ingredients: Over the liquids, evenly add the bread flour. Then, sprinkle the brown sugar and salt across the flour.
3. Add Pecans and Yeast: Distribute the chopped pecans over the other ingredients. Make a small well in the center of the dry ingredients (not too deep) and carefully add the yeast to the well, ensuring it does not come into direct contact with the liquids yet.
4. Select the Cycle: Set your bread maker to the Sweet Bread Cycle. This cycle is optimized for breads with sweeteners and additions like nuts, ensuring your Maple Pecan Bread comes out with a perfect texture and flavor.
5. Start the Bread Maker: Close the lid and start the cycle. The machine will handle the kneading, rising, and baking.
6. Cool Before Slicing: Once the baking cycle is complete, carefully remove the bread pan from the machine, and let the bread cool in the pan for about 10 minutes before transferring it to a wire rack to cool completely.
7. Serve: Slice the Maple Pecan Bread and enjoy it warm or at room temperature. It's delightful on its own, or you can serve it with additional maple syrup or butter for an extra indulgent treat.

Zucchini Bread

Prep: 15 Min

Serves: 1 loaf (8 to 10 slices)

Ingredient:

- 1 cup grated zucchini (about 1 medium zucchini, 225 g after grating and before squeezing out excess moisture)
- 2 large eggs
- ½ cup vegetable oil (120 ml)
- ½ cup sugar (100 g)
- ½ cup brown sugar (packed, 100 g)
- 1 teaspoon vanilla extract (5 ml)
- 2 cups all-purpose flour (256 g)
- 1 teaspoon ground cinnamon (2.6 g)
- ½ teaspoon baking powder (2.5 g)
- ½ teaspoon baking soda (2.5 g)
- ½ teaspoon salt (2.5 g)
- Optional: ½ cup chopped nuts or chocolate chips (75 g)

Instruction:

1. Prepare Zucchini: Grate the zucchini and lightly press it with a paper towel to remove excess moisture. Do not squeeze it dry; just remove the surface moisture.
2. Mix Wet Ingredients: In a bowl, beat together the eggs, vegetable oil, sugar, brown sugar, and vanilla extract until well combined. If your bread maker has a pre-mixing feature, you can also do this directly in the bread maker pan.
3. Add to Bread Maker: Pour the wet mixture into the bread maker pan. Then, add the grated zucchini on top.
4. Combine Dry Ingredients: In a separate bowl, whisk together the flour, cinnamon, baking powder, baking soda, and salt. Add this mixture over the wet ingredients in the bread maker pan. If using, sprinkle the optional nuts or chocolate chips last.
5. Choose the Sweet Bread or Cake Cycle on your bread maker.
6. Close the lid and start the selected cycle. The machine will mix the ingredients and bake the Zucchini Bread.
7. Once the cycle is complete, carefully remove the bread pan from the machine. Let the Zucchini Bread cool in the pan for about 10 minutes before transferring it to a wire rack to cool completely.
8. Serve: Slice the Zucchini Bread and enjoy. It's delicious as is, or you can serve it with butter, cream cheese, or your favorite spread.

CHAPTER 05: SWEET BREAD

Carrot Cake Bread

Prep: 15 Min

Serves: 1 loaf (8 to 10 slices)

Ingredient:

- 2 cups all-purpose flour (256 g)
- 2 teaspoons baking powder (10 g)
- 1/2 teaspoon baking soda (2.5 g)
- 1/4 teaspoon salt (1.25 g)
- 1 teaspoon ground cinnamon (2.6 g)
- 1/2 teaspoon ground nutmeg (1.2 g)
- 1/4 teaspoon ground ginger (0.6 g)
- 3/4 cup vegetable oil (180 ml)
- 1/4 cup unsweetened applesauce (60 ml) - to add moisture without too much extra fat
- 1 cup sugar (200 g)
- 3 large eggs
- 1 teaspoon vanilla extract (5 ml)
- 2 cups grated carrots (about 2 medium carrots, 240 g)
- 1/2 cup crushed pineapple, drained (about 120 ml after draining)
- 1/2 cup chopped walnuts or pecans (optional) (60 g)

Instruction:

1. Combine Dry Ingredients: In a large bowl, whisk together the flour, baking powder, baking soda, salt, cinnamon, nutmeg, and ginger. Set aside.
2. Mix Wet Ingredients: In another bowl, mix the vegetable oil, applesauce, sugar, eggs, and vanilla extract until well combined.
3. Add Wet Ingredients to Bread Maker: Pour the wet ingredient mixture into the bread maker pan.
4. Add Dry Ingredients: Carefully add the dry ingredient mixture over the wet ingredients in the bread maker pan.
5. Add Carrots and Pineapple: Evenly distribute the grated carrots and drained pineapple over the top. If using nuts, sprinkle them on last.
6. Set your bread maker to the Cake Cycle.
7. Close the lid and start the cycle. Scrape down the sides of the pan with a rubber spatula after the mixing begins, if necessary, to ensure all ingredients are incorporated.
8. Once the cycle is complete, carefully remove the pan from the bread maker. Let the Carrot Cake Bread cool in the pan for about 10 minutes before transferring it to a wire rack to cool completely.
9. Slice and serve the Carrot Cake Bread as is, or enhance it with a cream cheese frosting for an extra touch of sweetness.

Fig and Walnut Bread

Prep: 10   Min

Serves: 1 loaf (12 slices)

Ingredient:

- 1 cup water (240 ml), 80°F (27°C)
- 2 tablespoons olive oil (30 ml)
- 3 cups bread flour (381 g)
- 1/4 cup sugar (50 g)
- 1½ teaspoons salt (8.54 g)
- 1 cup dried figs, chopped (about 150 g)
- 3/4 cup walnuts, chopped (about 75 g)
- 1½ teaspoons active dry yeast (4.65 g)

Instruction:

1. Prepare Figs and Walnuts: Start by chopping the dried figs and walnuts into small, bite-sized pieces. This will ensure they are evenly distributed throughout the bread.
2. Add Liquids: Pour the water and olive oil into the bread maker pan.
3. Add Dry Ingredients: Over the liquids, evenly add the bread flour, then sprinkle the sugar and salt across the flour.
4. Make a Well for Yeast: Create a small well in the center of the dry ingredients (not too deep) and add the yeast to this well. This placement helps to keep the yeast separate from the liquids until the mixing starts.
5. Add Figs and Walnuts: Evenly distribute the chopped figs and walnuts on top of the flour. If your bread maker has a fruit and nut dispenser, use it to add these ingredients automatically at the right time during the kneading cycle; otherwise, add them at the beginning.
6. Choose the Sweet Bread Cycle on your bread maker.
7. Close the lid and start the selected cycle. The bread maker will mix, knead, rise, and bake the Fig and Walnut Bread.
8. Once the cycle is complete, carefully remove the bread pan from the machine. Let the bread cool in the pan for about 10 minutes before transferring it to a wire rack to cool completely.
9. Slice the Fig and Walnut Bread and enjoy it either as is, toasted, or with a spread of butter or cream cheese.

CHAPTER 05: SWEET BREAD

Cherry Almond Bread

Prep: 10   Min

Serves: 1 loaf (12 slices)

Ingredient:

- ¾ cup milk (180 ml), at room temperature
- ¼ cup unsalted butter, melted (60 ml)
- 2 large eggs
- ½ teaspoon almond extract (2.5 ml)
- 3 cups all-purpose flour (381 g)
- ½ cup sugar (100 g)
- 1½ teaspoons baking powder (7.5 g)
- ½ teaspoon salt (2.5 g)
- 1 cup dried cherries (150 g)
- ¾ cup sliced almonds (90 g)
- 1½ teaspoons active dry yeast (4.65 g)

Instruction:

1. In a bowl, whisk together the milk, melted butter, eggs, and almond extract.
2. Layer Ingredients in Bread Maker Pan: Pour the wet mixture into the bread maker pan. Then, gently add the flour, covering the liquid. Sprinkle the sugar, baking powder, and salt evenly over the flour.
3. Add Cherries and Almonds: Distribute the dried cherries and sliced almonds on top. If your bread maker has an add-in feature, follow the machine's prompts for adding these ingredients; otherwise, they can be added with the dry ingredients.
4. Add Yeast: If your cycle requires yeast, make a small well in the center of the dry ingredients (not too deep) and add the yeast.
5. Select the Cycle: Choose the Sweet Bread Cycle on your bread maker.
6. Close the lid and start the cycle. The machine will take care of the mixing, kneading, rising, and baking.
7. Once the baking cycle is complete, carefully remove the bread pan from the machine. Let the bread cool in the pan for about 10 minutes before transferring it to a wire rack to cool completely.
8. Slice the Cherry Almond Bread and enjoy. It's wonderful on its own or with a spread of almond butter or cream cheese.

Sweet Potato Bread

Prep: 15 Min

Serves: 1 loaf (12 slices)

Ingredient:

- 1 cup mashed sweet potato (about 1 medium sweet potato, 240 ml)
- 1/3 cup water (80 ml), 80°F (27°C)
- 1/4 cup unsalted butter, melted (60 ml)
- 1/4 cup milk (60 ml), 80°F (27°C)
- 2 tablespoons brown sugar (25 g)
- 1 teaspoon salt (5 g)
- 3 cups bread flour (381 g)
- 2 teaspoons ground cinnamon (5.2 g)
- 1/2 teaspoon ground nutmeg (1.2 g)
- 1½ teaspoons active dry yeast (4.65 g)

➤ Instruction:

1. Cook the sweet potato until tender (boiling or microwaving works well). Cool slightly, peel, and mash until smooth. Measure out 1 cup of mashed sweet potato.
2. Combine Wet Ingredients: In the bread maker pan, combine the mashed sweet potato, water, melted butter, and milk.
3. Add Dry Ingredients: Add the brown sugar, salt, bread flour, cinnamon, and nutmeg over the wet ingredients. Try to distribute them evenly across the pan.
4. Add Yeast: Make a small well in the center of the dry ingredients (not too deep) and add the yeast to this well, ensuring it doesn't touch the wet ingredients directly.
5. Choose the Sweet Bread Cycle on your bread maker.
6. Close the lid and start the selected cycle. The bread maker will take care of the mixing, kneading, rising, and baking processes.
7. Once the cycle is complete, carefully remove the bread pan from the machine, and allow the bread to cool in the pan for about 10 minutes before transferring it to a wire rack to cool completely.
8. Slice the Sweet Potato Bread and enjoy it warm or at room temperature. It's delicious on its own, with butter, or as a base for sandwiches.

CHAPTER 05: SWEET BREAD

Date and Honey Bread

Prep: 10 Min

Serves: 1 loaf (12 slices)

Ingredient:

- 1 cup water (240 ml), 80°F (27°C)
- 1/4 cup honey (60 ml)
- 2 tablespoons unsalted butter, melted (30 ml)
- 3 cups bread flour (381 g)
- 1/4 cup milk powder (30 g)
- 2 tablespoons sugar (25 g)
- 1 teaspoon salt (5 g)
- 1 cup dates, pitted and chopped (about 160 g)
- 1½ teaspoons active dry yeast (4.65 g)

➤ Instruction:

1. Start by chopping the pitted dates into small pieces to ensure they are evenly distributed throughout the bread.
2. Combine Liquids: In the bread maker pan, combine the water, honey, and melted butter.
3. Add Dry Ingredients: Over the liquids, evenly add the bread flour, milk powder, sugar, and salt.
4. Add Dates: Distribute the chopped dates over the flour. If your bread maker has a fruit and nut dispenser, use it to add the dates at the correct time during the kneading process; otherwise, add them at the beginning.
5. Make a Well for Yeast: Create a small well in the center of the dry ingredients (not too deep) and add the yeast to this well, ensuring it doesn't touch the wet ingredients directly.
6. Choose the Sweet Bread Cycle on your bread maker.
7. Close the lid and start the selected cycle. The machine will take care of the mixing, kneading, rising, and baking processes.
8. Once the cycle is complete, carefully remove the bread pan from the machine, and let the bread cool in the pan for about 10 minutes before transferring it to a wire rack to cool completely.
9. Slice the Date and Honey Bread and enjoy it warm or at room temperature. It's particularly delicious when served with butter or as a base for French toast.

Apricot Bread

Prep: 10 Min

Serves: 1 loaf (12 slices)

Ingredient:

- 1 cup water (240 ml), 80°F (27°C)
- ¼ cup apricot nectar (60 ml)
- 2 tablespoons unsalted butter, melted (30 ml)
- 3 cups bread flour (381 g)
- ¼ cup sugar (50 g)
- 1½ teaspoons salt (8.54 g)
- ¾ cup dried apricots, chopped (about 120 g)
- 1½ teaspoons active dry yeast (4.65 g)

 ## Instruction:

1. Start by chopping the dried apricots into small, bite-sized pieces. This ensures they are evenly distributed throughout the bread.
2. Add Liquids to Bread Maker Pan: Pour the water, apricot nectar, and melted butter into the bread maker pan.
3. Add Dry Ingredients: Over the liquids, evenly add the bread flour. Then, sprinkle the sugar and salt across the flour.
4. Add Apricots: Distribute the chopped dried apricots over the flour. If your bread maker has a fruit and nut dispenser, add the apricots there; otherwise, include them with the other ingredients so they are mixed throughout the dough.
5. Create a small well in the center of the dry ingredients (not too deep) and add the yeast to this well, ensuring it doesn't touch the liquids directly.
6. Choose the Sweet Bread Cycle on your bread maker.
7. Close the lid and start the selected cycle. The bread maker will take care of mixing, kneading, rising, and baking the Apricot Bread.
8. Once the cycle is complete, carefully remove the bread pan from the machine. Allow the bread to cool in the pan for about 10 minutes before transferring it to a wire rack to cool completely.
9. Slice the Apricot Bread and enjoy it either warm or at room temperature. It pairs beautifully with butter, cream cheese, or even a light apricot glaze for an extra touch of sweetness.

CHAPTER 05: SWEET BREAD

Lemon Poppy Seed Bread

Prep: 10 Min

Serves: 1 loaf (12 slices)

Ingredient:

- ¾ cup milk (180 ml), 80°F (27°C)
- ¼ cup unsalted butter, melted (60 ml)
- 3 tablespoons lemon juice (45 ml)
- 2 large eggs
- 3 cups bread flour (381 g)
- ¾ cup sugar (150 g)
- 1½ teaspoons salt (8.54 g)
- 2 tablespoons poppy seeds (18 g)
- Zest of 2 large lemons (about 2 tablespoons or 6 g)
- 1½ teaspoons active dry yeast (4.65 g)

Instruction:

1. Zest the lemons to get about 2 tablespoons of lemon zest. Juice the lemons to get 3 tablespoons of lemon juice.
2. Combine Wet Ingredients: In the bread maker pan, combine the milk, melted butter, lemon juice, and eggs.
3. Add Dry Ingredients: Over the wet ingredients, evenly add the bread flour. Then, sprinkle the sugar and salt across the flour. Add the lemon zest and poppy seeds, distributing them evenly.
4. Make a Well for Yeast: Create a small well in the center of the dry ingredients (not too deep) and add the yeast to this well, ensuring it doesn't touch the liquids directly.
5. Choose the Sweet Bread Cycle on your bread maker.
6. Close the lid and start the selected cycle. The machine will take care of the mixing, kneading, rising, and baking processes.
7. Once the cycle is complete, carefully remove the bread pan from the machine, and let the bread cool in the pan for about 10 minutes before transferring it to a wire rack to cool completely.
8. Slice the Lemon Poppy Seed Bread and enjoy it warm or at room temperature. It's delightful on its own, with a spread of butter, or topped with a simple lemon glaze for an extra burst of lemon flavor.

Strawberry Bread

Prep: 10 Min

Serves: 1 loaf (12 slices)

Ingredient:

- ¾ cup milk (180 ml), 80°F (27°C)
- ¼ cup vegetable oil (60 ml)
- 1 large egg
- ½ cup sugar (100 g)
- 1 teaspoon vanilla extract (5 ml)
- 3 cups bread flour (381 g)
- 1½ teaspoons baking powder (7.5 g)
- ½ teaspoon salt (2.5 g)
- 1 cup fresh strawberries, chopped (about 150 g)
- 1½ teaspoons active dry yeast (4.65 g)

Instruction:

1. Rinse the strawberries, hull them, and chop into small pieces. If you prefer, you can lightly coat them in flour to help distribute them evenly in the batter and prevent sinking.
2. Combine Wet Ingredients: In the bread maker pan, whisk together the milk, vegetable oil, egg, sugar, and vanilla extract.
3. Add Dry Ingredients: Over the wet mixture, add the bread flour, baking powder, and salt. If your bread maker cycle includes yeast and is designed for such recipes, make a small well in the center of the dry ingredients and add the yeast.
4. Add Strawberries: Distribute the chopped strawberries over the top of the dry ingredients. If your bread maker has an add-in feature, use it as directed; otherwise, add the strawberries at the beginning.
5. Choose the Sweet Bread Cycle on your bread maker.
6. Close the lid and start the selected cycle. The machine will take care of the mixing, kneading, rising, and baking processes.
7. Once the cycle is complete, carefully remove the bread pan from the machine, and let the bread cool in the pan for about 10 minutes before transferring it to a wire rack to cool completely.
8. Slice the Strawberry Bread and enjoy it warm or at room temperature. It's delicious on its own, with a spread of cream cheese, or topped with a simple glaze for added sweetness.

CHAPTER 05: SWEET BREAD

Pineapple Bread

Prep: 5 Min

Serves: 1 loaf (12 slices)

Ingredient:

- ¾ cup pineapple juice (180 ml), 80°F (27°C)
- ¼ cup unsalted butter, melted (60 ml)
- ½ cup sugar (100 g)
- 1 teaspoon vanilla extract (5 ml)
- 3 cups bread flour (381 g)
- 1½ teaspoons active dry yeast (4.65 g)
- 1 cup crushed pineapple, drained (about 225 g)
- Optional: ½ cup shredded coconut (40 g) for added tropical flavor.

Instruction:

1. Add Liquids: In the bread maker pan, combine the pineapple juice, melted butter, and vanilla extract.
2. Add Dry Ingredients: Over the liquids, evenly add the bread flour and sugar. Make a small well in the center of the dry ingredients and add the yeast to this well.
3. Add Pineapple (and Coconut): Evenly distribute the crushed pineapple (and shredded coconut, if using) over the top of the flour. If your bread maker has a mix-in feature, add the pineapple at the signal; otherwise, add it at the beginning to ensure it's well incorporated.
4. Choose the Sweet Bread Cycle on your bread maker.
5. Close the lid and start the selected cycle. The machine will take care of the mixing, kneading, rising, and baking processes.
6. Once the baking cycle is complete, carefully remove the bread pan from the machine, and let the bread cool in the pan for about 10 minutes before transferring it to a wire rack to cool completely.
7. Slice the Pineapple Bread and enjoy it warm or at room temperature. It's delicious on its own, with a spread of butter, or even toasted with a little honey for extra sweetness.

Panettone

Prep: 10 Min

Serves: 1 loaf (12 slices)

Ingredient:

- ⅔ cup milk (160 ml), 80°F (27°C)
- 2 large eggs, beaten
- ¼ cup unsalted butter, melted (60 ml)
- ½ cup sugar (100 g)
- ½ teaspoon salt (2.5 g)
- 3 cups bread flour (381 g)
- 1 tablespoon orange zest (6 g)
- 1½ teaspoons active dry yeast (4.65 g)
- ½ cup raisins (80 g)
- ½ cup mixed candied fruit (80 g)

➤ Instruction:

1. Ensure the milk is warmed to about 80°F (27°C). Lightly beat the eggs. Melt the butter and let it cool slightly. Prepare the orange zest, and gather the raisins and mixed candied fruit.
2. Add Liquids to Bread Maker Pan: Pour the milk into the bread maker pan. Add the beaten eggs and melted butter.
3. Add Dry Ingredients: Over the liquids, evenly add the sugar, salt, and bread flour. Sprinkle the orange zest over the flour. Make a small well in the center of the dry ingredients and add the yeast to this well.
4. Add Fruit: If your bread maker has an add-in feature, add the raisins and mixed candied fruit at the signal; otherwise, add them at the beginning to ensure they're mixed throughout the dough.
5. Choose the Sweet Bread Cycle on your bread maker.
6. Close the lid and start the selected cycle. The bread maker will handle the mixing, kneading, rising, and baking processes.
7. Once the baking cycle is complete, carefully remove the bread pan from the machine, and let the Panettone cool in the pan for about 10 minutes before transferring it to a wire rack to cool completely.
8. Slice the Panettone and enjoy it warm or at room temperature. It's delightful on its own, with coffee or tea, or as part of a holiday breakfast or dessert.

CHAPTER 06: HOLIDAY BREAD

Stollen

Prep: 15 Min

Serves: 1 large loaf or 2 smaller loaves

Ingredient:

- ½ cup milk (120 ml), 80°F (27°C)
- 2 large eggs, room temperature
- ¼ cup unsalted butter, melted (60 ml)
- ¼ cup sugar (50 g)
- 1 teaspoon salt (5 g)
- 2½ cups bread flour (318 g)
- 1 teaspoon ground cinnamon (2.6 g)
- 2 teaspoons active dry yeast (6.4 g)
- 1 cup mixed dried fruits (raisins, currants, chopped apricots, cranberries) (160 g)
- ½ cup chopped almonds or walnuts (65 g)
- Optional: ¼ cup candied orange or lemon peel (40 g)
- Marzipan or almond paste, for filling (about 100 g)

➤ Instruction:

1. Add the milk, eggs, melted butter, sugar, and salt to the bread maker pan.
2. Add the bread flour over the wet ingredients. Sprinkle the ground cinnamon around and make a small well in the center for the yeast. Add the yeast to the well.
3. Select the Dough Cycle on your bread maker and start it. The machine will mix, knead, and perform the first rise of the dough.
4. Add Fruits and Nuts: If your bread maker has an add-in feature, use it to add the mixed dried fruits, nuts, and optional candied peel at the signal. Otherwise, pause the machine towards the end of the kneading phase to incorporate them manually, then resume the cycle.
5. Prepare Marzipan: While the dough is being prepared, roll your marzipan or almond paste into a log or two smaller logs if making two loaves.
6. Shape and Fill Dough: Once the Dough Cycle is complete, turn the dough out onto a lightly floured surface. Roll out to a large rectangle (or two rectangles if dividing). Place the marzipan log(s) in the center and fold the dough over it, sealing the marzipan inside.
7. Place the shaped dough on a baking sheet lined with parchment paper. Cover loosely with a clean kitchen towel and let rise in a warm place for about 30 minutes, or until roughly doubled in size.
8. Preheat your oven to 350°F (175°C). Once preheated, bake the Stollen for 30-40 minutes, or until golden brown and a skewer inserted into the center comes out clean.
9. Let the Stollen cool on a wire rack. Once cooled, dust generously with powdered sugar to decorate. Slice the Stollen and enjoy.

Rosca de Reyes

Prep: 15 Min

Serves: 1 Rosca de Reyes
(approximately 12 slices)

Ingredient:

- ½ cup milk (120 ml), 80°F (27°C)
- ¼ cup unsalted butter, melted (60 ml)
- 3 large eggs, beaten
- ¼ cup sugar (50 g)
- Zest of 1 orange (about 1 tablespoon or 6 g)
- ½ teaspoon salt (2.5 g)
- 3 cups bread flour (381 g)
- 2 teaspoons active dry yeast (6.4 g)
- 1 teaspoon ground cinnamon (2.6 g)
- ½ cup mixed candied fruits (chopped) (80 g)
- Optional: 1 or 2 small figurines to hide in the bread after baking

Instruction:

1. Combine the milk, melted butter, and beaten eggs in the bread maker pan.
2. Add Dry Ingredients: Over the wet ingredients, evenly add the sugar, orange zest, salt, bread flour, cinnamon, and finally the yeast. Make a small well in the center of the flour for the yeast.
3. Choose the Sweet Bread Cycle on your bread maker.
4. Add Candied Fruits: If your bread maker has an add-in feature, add the chopped mixed candied fruits at the signal; otherwise, incorporate them at the beginning to ensure they're evenly distributed through the dough.
5. Close the lid and start the selected cycle. The machine will mix, knead, rise, and bake the Rosca de Reyes.
6. Once the cycle is complete, carefully remove the bread pan from the machine. If you're adding figurines, now is the time to gently press them into the bottom of the bread. Let the Rosca cool in the pan for about 10 minutes before transferring it to a wire rack to cool completely.
7. Traditionally, Rosca de Reyes is decorated with more candied fruits on top. You can brush the top with a little warmed apricot jam or honey and arrange additional candied fruits for decoration.
8. Slice the Rosca de Reyes and serve. It's typically enjoyed with hot chocolate or coffee.

CHAPTER 06: HOLIDAY BREAD

Kugelhopf

Prep: 20 Min

Serves: 1 Kugelhopf (approximately 12 slices)

Ingredient:

- ½ cup milk (120 ml), warmed to 80°F (27°C)
- 3 large eggs, lightly beaten
- ¼ cup melted butter (60 ml)
- ¼ cup sugar (50 g)
- ½ teaspoon salt (2.5 g)
- 1 teaspoon vanilla extract (5 ml)
- 3 cups bread flour (381 g)
- 2 teaspoons active dry yeast (6.4 g)
- ½ cup raisins (80 g), soaked in rum or warm water for 15 minutes and drained
- ½ cup chopped almonds (60 g)
- Zest of 1 lemon (about 1 tablespoon or 6 g)
- Optional for serving: Powdered sugar for dusting

Instruction:

1. Soak the raisins in rum or warm water to plump them up, then drain. Warm the milk to the specified temperature.
2. Add Wet Ingredients to Pan: Pour the warmed milk, beaten eggs, melted butter, and vanilla extract into the bread maker pan.
3. Add Dry Ingredients: Over the wet ingredients, evenly add the sugar, salt, and bread flour. Sprinkle the lemon zest around the flour. Make a small well in the center of the flour and add the yeast to this well.
4. Add Raisins and Almonds: If your bread maker has an add-in feature, use it for the raisins and chopped almonds; otherwise, add them at the beginning to ensure they're incorporated throughout the dough.
5. Select the Cycle: Choose the Sweet Bread or Cake Cycle on your bread maker.
6. Close the lid and start the selected cycle. The machine will take care of the rest, perfectly baking your Kugelhopf.
7. Once the cycle is complete, carefully remove the bread pan from the machine. Let the Kugelhopf cool in the pan for about 10 minutes before transferring it to a wire rack to cool completely.
8. Once cooled, dust the Kugelhopf with powdered sugar for a traditional finish. Slice and serve as part of your breakfast, brunch, or tea time.

Julekake

Prep: 10 Min

Serves: 1 loaf (12 slices)

Ingredient:

- ¾ cup milk (180 ml), 80°F (27°C)
- ¼ cup unsalted butter, melted (60 ml)
- 1 large egg
- ¼ cup sugar (50 g)
- ½ teaspoon salt (2.5 g)
- 3 cups bread flour (381 g)
- 1½ teaspoons active dry yeast (4.65 g)
- 1 teaspoon ground cardamom (2 g)
- ¾ cup mixed candied fruit and raisins (120 g)
- Optional: ¼ cup chopped almonds (30 g)

Instruction:

1. Start by pouring the milk into the bread maker pan. Add the melted butter and the egg. If your bread maker has specific instructions for adding liquids and eggs, follow those to ensure the best results.
2. Add Dry Ingredients: Sprinkle the sugar, salt, and ground cardamom over the liquid ingredients. Carefully add the bread flour, covering the liquid. Make a small well in the center of the flour and add the yeast to this well, ensuring it does not touch the liquid directly.
3. Add Fruits and Nuts: Evenly distribute the mixed candied fruit, raisins, and optional chopped almonds on top of the flour. If your bread maker has an add-in feature, follow the machine's prompts for adding these ingredients; otherwise, add them at the beginning to ensure they're well incorporated.
4. Choose the Sweet Bread Cycle on your bread maker.
5. Close the lid and start the selected cycle. The bread maker will mix, knead, rise, and bake the Julekake.
6. Once the baking cycle is complete, carefully remove the bread pan from the machine, and let the Julekake cool in the pan for about 10 minutes before transferring it to a wire rack to cool completely.
7. Slice the Julekake and enjoy it warm or at room temperature. It's traditionally served with butter, cheese, or even jam for a festive treat.

CHAPTER 06: HOLIDAY BREAD

Vánočka

Prep: 20 Min

Serves: 1 large loaf

Ingredient:

- 1 cup milk (240 ml), warmed to 80°F (27°C)
- 2 large eggs, beaten (reserve a little for egg wash)
- ¼ cup unsalted butter, melted (60 ml)
- ½ cup sugar (100 g)
- ½ teaspoon salt (2.5 g)
- 4 cups bread flour (508 g)
- 2 teaspoons active dry yeast (6.4 g)
- 1 teaspoon lemon zest (about 2 g)
- ½ cup raisins (80 g), soaked in warm water and drained
- ¼ cup almonds, chopped (30 g)
- Optional: ¼ cup candied fruit (40 g)

Instruction:

1. Warm the milk to about 80°F (27°C). Beat the eggs (reserve a bit for an egg wash later). Soak the raisins in warm water, then drain.
2. Add Ingredients to Bread Maker: Pour the warm milk, beaten eggs (less the reserved amount for egg wash), and melted butter into the bread maker pan. Add the sugar, salt, and lemon zest. Evenly distribute the bread flour over the liquids. Make a small indentation in the flour and add the yeast to this indentation.
3. Add the drained raisins, chopped almonds, and optional candied fruit to the bread maker if it has a fruit/nut dispenser. Otherwise, add them after the initial mixing. Select the Dough Cycle and start the bread maker.
4. Once the Dough Cycle is complete, remove the dough and divide it into three equal parts for a simple braid (or more parts for a traditional multi-layered braid). Roll each part into a long strand and braid them together. Place the braided dough on a baking sheet lined with parchment paper.
5. Cover the braided dough with a clean kitchen towel and let it rise in a warm place until doubled in size, about 45 minutes to 1 hour.
6. Preheat Oven: While the dough is rising, preheat your oven to 350°F (175°C).
7. Brush the risen dough with the reserved beaten egg. Sprinkle the top with additional almonds or sugar if desired. Bake the Vánočka in the preheated oven for 25-30 minutes, or until it's golden brown and sounds hollow when tapped on the bottom. If the top browns too quickly, cover it with aluminum foil.
8. Remove the Vánočka from the oven and let it cool on a wire rack before slicing.

Christmas Fruit Bread

Prep: 10   Min

Serves: 1 loaf (12 slices)

Ingredient:

- ¾ cup lukewarm water (180 ml), 80°F (27°C)
- ¼ cup orange juice (60 ml), 80°F (27°C)
- 2 tablespoons unsalted butter, melted (30 ml)
- 3 cups bread flour (381 g)
- ½ cup sugar (100 g)
- 1 teaspoon salt (5 g)
- 2 teaspoons ground cinnamon (5.2 g)
- 1½ teaspoons active dry yeast (4.65 g)
- 1 cup mixed dried fruits (raisins, currants, chopped apricots, and cranberries) (160 g)
- ½ cup chopped mixed nuts (walnuts, almonds) (60 g)
- Optional: Zest of 1 orange (about 1 tablespoon or 6 g) for added flavor

 ## Instruction:

1. Pour the lukewarm water and orange juice into the bread maker pan. Add the melted butter.
2. Add Dry Ingredients: Over the liquids, evenly add the bread flour, sugar, salt, and cinnamon. Make a small well in the center of the flour and add the yeast to this well, ensuring it does not touch the liquid directly.
3. Add Fruits, Nuts, and Zest: Evenly distribute the mixed dried fruits, chopped nuts, and optional orange zest over the top. If your bread maker has a fruit and nut dispenser, use it to add these ingredients at the correct time; otherwise, add them at the beginning to ensure they're mixed throughout the dough.
4. Choose the Sweet Bread Cycle on your bread maker.
5. Close the lid and start the selected cycle. The machine will take care of the mixing, kneading, rising, and baking processes.
6. Once the baking cycle is complete, carefully remove the bread pan from the machine, and let the Christmas Fruit Bread cool in the pan for about 10 minutes before transferring it to a wire rack to cool completely.
7. Slice the Christmas Fruit Bread and enjoy it warm or at room temperature. It's delicious on its own, with butter, or as part of a festive holiday breakfast or tea time.

CHAPTER 06: HOLIDAY BREAD

Saffron Bread

Prep: 15   Min

Serves: 1 loaf (12 slices)

Ingredient:

- 1 cup warm milk (240 ml), 80°F (27°C) — infused with a generous pinch of saffron threads
- 2 tablespoons unsalted butter, melted (30 ml)
- 1 large egg, beaten
- ¼ cup sugar (50 g)
- ½ teaspoon salt (2.5 g)
- 3½ cups bread flour (445 g)
- 1½ teaspoons active dry yeast (4.65 g)
- ½ cup raisins (80 g), optional
- ½ cup dried currants or chopped dried apricots (80 g), optional

Instruction:

1. Warm the milk to about 80°F (27°C) and infuse it with a generous pinch of saffron threads for at least 10 minutes. The milk will take on a vibrant golden color.
2. Combine Wet Ingredients: Pour the saffron-infused milk into the bread maker pan. Add the melted butter and beaten egg.
3. Add Dry Ingredients: Over the wet ingredients, evenly add the sugar, salt, and bread flour. Make a small well in the center of the flour and add the yeast to this well.
4. Add Fruits: If using, add the raisins and dried currants or chopped dried apricots. If your bread maker has an add-in feature, use it for adding the fruits at the correct time; otherwise, add them at the beginning to ensure they're evenly distributed.
5. Select the Cycle: Choose the Sweet Bread Cycle on your bread maker.
6. Close the lid and start the selected cycle. The machine will take care of mixing, kneading, rising, and baking the Saffron Bread.
7. Once the cycle is complete, carefully remove the bread pan from the machine. Let the bread cool in the pan for about 10 minutes before transferring it to a wire rack to cool completely.
8. Slice the Saffron Bread and enjoy it warm or at room temperature. It pairs wonderfully with butter or jam for breakfast or as a special treat during the holidays.

Bolo Rei

Prep: 20 Min

Serves: 1 Bolo Rei (approximately 12 slices)

Ingredient:

- ¾ cup lukewarm milk (180 ml), 80°F (27°C)
- 3 tablespoons unsalted butter, melted (45 ml)
- 3 large eggs, beaten
- ½ cup sugar (100 g)
- ½ teaspoon salt (2.5 g)
- 3½ cups bread flour (445 g)
- 1½ teaspoons active dry yeast (4.65 g)
- Zest of 1 lemon (about 1 tablespoon or 6 g)
- Zest of 1 orange (about 1 tablespoon or 6 g)
- ½ cup mixed candied fruit (80 g), plus extra for topping
- ¼ cup raisins (40 g)
- ¼ cup chopped nuts (walnuts, almonds, or pecans) (30 g)
- Optional: 1 fava bean or small toy for tradition

Instruction:

1. Add the lukewarm milk, melted butter, beaten eggs, sugar, and salt to the bread maker pan. Then, add the bread flour. Sprinkle the lemon and orange zest over the flour. Make a small indentation in the flour and add the yeast to this indentation. Select the Dough Cycle and start the bread maker.
2. Add Fruits and Nuts: If your bread maker has a fruit and nut dispenser, use it for the mixed candied fruit, raisins, and chopped nuts. Otherwise, add them towards the end of the kneading process.
3. Once the Dough Cycle is complete, remove the dough from the bread maker. On a lightly floured surface, shape the dough into a large ring, placing a greased proofing ring or a small bowl in the center to maintain the shape if needed. If following tradition, hide a fava bean or a small toy inside the dough.
4. Place the shaped dough on a baking sheet lined with parchment paper. Cover with a clean cloth and let it rise in a warm place until doubled in size, about 1 hour.
5. Preheat your oven to 350°F (175°C). Brush the dough with a beaten egg or milk for a glossy finish. Decorate the top with additional candied fruit and nuts.
6. Bake the Bolo Rei in the preheated oven for 25-30 minutes, or until golden brown and cooked through. If the cake is browning too quickly, cover it with aluminum foil.
7. Cool and Serve: Let the Bolo Rei cool on a wire rack before serving. Dust with powdered sugar if desired.

CHAPTER 06: HOLIDAY BREAD

Challah

Prep: 10 Min

Serves: 1 large loaf

Ingredient:

- 1 cup warm water (240 ml), 80°F (27°C)
- 2 large eggs, plus 1 for egg wash
- ¼ cup olive oil (60 ml)
- 4 cups bread flour (508 g)
- ¼ cup sugar (50 g)
- 1½ teaspoons salt (8.54 g)
- 2 teaspoons active dry yeast (6.4 g)

Instruction:

1. Pour the warm water into the bread maker pan. Add the 2 beaten eggs and olive oil. Next, add the bread flour, ensuring it covers the liquid. Sprinkle the sugar and salt evenly over the flour. Make a small indentation in the center of the flour and add the yeast to this indentation.
2. Start Dough Cycle: Select the Dough Cycle on your bread maker and start the machine. The bread maker will mix, knead, and undergo the first rise of the dough.
3. Braid the Dough: Once the Dough Cycle is complete, remove the dough from the bread maker. On a lightly floured surface, divide the dough into three (or more, depending on your preferred braid) equal parts. Roll each part into a long strand and braid them together. Place the braided dough on a baking sheet lined with parchment paper.
4. Second Rise: Cover the braided dough with a clean kitchen towel and let it rise in a warm place until nearly doubled in size, about 30-60 minutes.
5. Preheat your oven to 375°F (190°C).
6. Beat the remaining egg and brush it over the top of the risen dough to create a shiny, golden crust.
7. Bake the Challah in the preheated oven for 25-30 minutes, or until it's golden brown and sounds hollow when tapped on the bottom.
8. Remove the Challah from the oven and let it cool on a wire rack before slicing.

Pulla

Prep: 10 Min

Serves: 1 large loaf or several smaller braids

Ingredient:

- 1 cup warm milk (240 ml), 80°F (27°C)
- ¼ cup unsalted butter, melted (60 ml)
- 1 large egg, beaten
- ¼ cup sugar (50 g)
- 1 teaspoon salt (5 g)
- 1 tablespoon ground cardamom (6 g)
- 4 cups bread flour (508 g)
- 2 teaspoons active dry yeast (6.4 g)
- Optional: Pearl sugar or sliced almonds for topping

Instruction:

1. Pour the warm milk into the bread maker pan. Add the melted butter, beaten egg, sugar, salt, and ground cardamom. Next, add the bread flour, covering the wet ingredients. Make a small well in the center of the flour and add the yeast.
2. Select the Dough Cycle on your bread maker and start the machine. The bread maker will mix, knead, and rise the dough.
3. Once the Dough Cycle is complete, remove the dough from the bread maker. On a lightly floured surface, divide the dough as desired (into three strands for a braid, or into smaller pieces for individual rolls). Braid or shape the dough and place it on a baking sheet lined with parchment paper. If making a braid, you can tuck the ends under for a neat finish.
4. Cover the shaped dough with a clean kitchen towel and let it rise in a warm place until nearly doubled in size, about 30-60 minutes.
5. Preheat your oven to 375°F (190°C).
6. Brush the risen dough with a mixture of beaten egg and water (for shine) and sprinkle with pearl sugar or sliced almonds if using.
7. Bake the Pulla in the preheated oven for 20-25 minutes, or until golden brown and the bottom sounds hollow when tapped. Larger loaves may require additional baking time.
8. Remove the Pulla from the oven and let it cool on a wire rack before slicing.

CHAPTER 06: HOLIDAY BREAD

Cozonac

Prep: 20 Min

Serves: 2 loaves

Ingredient:

- 1 cup warm milk (240 ml), 80°F (27°C)
- 2 large eggs, beaten
- ½ cup sugar (100 g)
- ½ cup unsalted butter, melted (120 ml)
- 4½ cups bread flour (572 g)
- 2 teaspoons active dry yeast (6.4 g)
- Zest of 1 lemon
- Zest of 1 orange
- 1 teaspoon vanilla extract (5 ml)
- ½ teaspoon salt (2.5 g)

For the Walnut Filling:

- 2 cups ground walnuts (200 g)
- ½ cup sugar (100 g)
- ¼ cup cocoa powder (optional) (25 g)
- ½ cup milk (120 ml)
- 1 teaspoon vanilla extract (5 ml)

Instruction:

1. In the bread maker pan, combine the warm milk, beaten eggs, sugar, melted butter, bread flour, yeast, lemon zest, orange zest, vanilla extract, and salt. Select the Dough Cycle and start the machine.
2. Make the Filling: While the dough is kneading, prepare the filling. In a saucepan over medium heat, combine the ground walnuts, sugar, cocoa powder (if using), milk, and vanilla extract. Cook, stirring constantly, until the mixture thickens. Remove from heat and let cool.
3. Once the Dough Cycle is complete, divide the dough into two equal parts. On a lightly floured surface, roll out each part into a rectangle. Spread half of the walnut filling over each rectangle, leaving a small border around the edges.
4. Roll each rectangle tightly from one of the long edges, then twist the roll to ensure the filling is evenly distributed. Place each twisted roll into a greased loaf pan.
5. Cover the loaf pans with a clean kitchen towel and let them rise in a warm place until doubled in size, about 1 hour.
6. Preheat your oven to 350°F (175°C).
7. Brush the top of each loaf with beaten egg or milk for a glossy finish. Bake in the preheated oven for 35-40 minutes, or until the Cozonac is golden brown and sounds hollow when tapped on the bottom.
8. Remove the Cozonac from the oven and let it cool in the pans for about 10 minutes, then transfer to a wire rack to cool completely.

Chocolate Babka

Prep: 20 Min

Serves: 1 large babka or 2 smaller loaves

Ingredient:

Dough Ingredients:
- ¾ cup milk (180 ml), warmed to 27°C (80°F)
- 2 large eggs, room temperature
- ¼ cup unsalted butter, melted (60 ml)
- ¼ cup sugar (50 g)
- ½ teaspoon salt (2.5 g)
- 3 cups bread flour (381 g)
- 2 teaspoons active dry yeast (6.4 g)

Chocolate Filling:
- ½ cup unsalted butter (115 g), room temperature
- 1 cup sugar (200 g)
- ½ cup unsweetened cocoa powder (50 g)
- Optional: 1 cup chocolate chips (160 g) for extra chocolatey filling

➤ Instruction:

1. Place the warm milk, melted butter, beaten eggs, sugar, and salt into the bread maker pan. Add the bread flour on top. Make a small well in the center of the flour and add the yeast. Select the Dough Cycle and start the bread maker.
2. While the dough is kneading, prepare the filling by mixing the room temperature butter, sugar, and cocoa powder until well combined. If using, stir in the chocolate chips.
3. Once the Dough Cycle is complete, turn the dough out onto a lightly floured surface. Roll the dough into a large rectangle about ¼ inch thick. Spread the chocolate filling evenly over the dough, leaving a small border around the edges.
4. Roll the dough tightly from one of the long edges, then cut the log in half lengthwise, leaving one end attached. Twist the two halves together, keeping the cut sides facing up. Transfer to a greased loaf pan.
5. Cover the loaf pan with a clean kitchen towel and let the babka rise in a warm place until puffed, about 1 hour.
6. Preheat your oven to 175°C (350°F).
7. Bake the babka in the preheated oven for 30-35 minutes, or until it has risen and the top is golden brown. If the babka is browning too quickly, tent it with aluminum foil.
8. Allow the babka to cool in the pan for about 10 minutes, then transfer it to a wire rack to cool completely before slicing. Slice the babka and serve.

CHAPTER 06: HOLIDAY BREAD

Hot Cross Buns

Prep: 10 Min   Serves: 12 buns

Ingredient:

Ingredients for the Dough:
- 1 cup milk (240 ml), warmed to 80°F (27°C)
- ¼ cup unsalted butter, melted (60 ml)
- 1 large egg
- ¼ cup sugar (50 g)
- ½ teaspoon salt (2.5 g)
- 1 teaspoon ground cinnamon (2.6 g)
- ¼ teaspoon ground nutmeg (0.5 g)
- 3 cups bread flour (381 g)
- 1 tablespoon active dry yeast (9.45 g)
- ¾ cup raisins or mixed dried fruit (120 g)

Ingredients for the Cross:
- ½ cup all-purpose flour (60 g)
- 5 tablespoons water (approximately 75 ml)
- Ingredients for the Glaze:
- ¼ cup granulated sugar (50 g)
- 2 tablespoons water

➤ Instruction:

1. Add the warm milk, melted butter, beaten egg, sugar, salt, cinnamon, nutmeg, and bread flour to the bread maker pan in that order. Make a small indentation in the flour and add the yeast. Select the Dough Cycle and start the machine. Add the raisins or mixed dried fruit when there's about 5-10 minutes left in the kneading cycle or at the beep for adding ingredients.
2. Once the Dough Cycle is complete, turn the dough out onto a lightly floured surface. Divide the dough into 12 equal pieces and shape each piece into a smooth ball. Place the balls of dough on a baking sheet lined with parchment paper, leaving space between each for expansion.
3. Mix the all-purpose flour with enough water to make a thick paste. Spoon the paste into a piping bag or a plastic bag with a small corner cut off and pipe crosses onto each bun.
4. Cover the buns with a clean kitchen towel and let them rise in a warm place until nearly doubled in size, about 30-45 minutes.
5. Preheat your oven to 375°F (190°C). Bake the hot cross buns for 20-25 minutes, or until they are golden brown.
6. While the buns are baking, heat the granulated sugar and water in a small saucepan until the sugar is dissolved and the mixture is syrupy.
7. Brush the warm glaze over the hot buns as soon as they come out of the oven. Let the hot cross buns cool on a wire rack. Serve warm or at room temperature.

Gingerbread Loaf

Prep: 10 Min

Serves: 1 loaf (8-10 slices)

Ingredient:

- ½ cup milk (120 ml), 80°F (27°C)
- ½ cup unsulfured molasses (120 ml)
- ¼ cup unsalted butter, melted (60 ml)
- 1 large egg
- ½ cup brown sugar (100 g)
- 2 cups all-purpose flour (240 g)
- 1 teaspoon baking powder (4 g)
- ½ teaspoon baking soda (2.5 g)
- ½ teaspoon salt (2.5 g)
- 1 tablespoon ground ginger (6 g)
- 1 teaspoon ground cinnamon (2.6 g)
- ¼ teaspoon ground cloves (0.5 g)
- ¼ teaspoon ground nutmeg (0.5 g)

Instruction:

1. Combine Wet Ingredients: In a medium bowl, whisk together the milk, molasses, melted butter, and egg until well combined.
2. Add to Bread Maker: Pour the wet ingredients into the bread maker pan.
3. Mix Dry Ingredients: In another bowl, mix together the brown sugar, all-purpose flour, baking powder, baking soda, salt, ginger, cinnamon, cloves, and nutmeg.
4. Add Dry Ingredients to Pan: Carefully add the mixed dry ingredients over the wet ingredients in the bread maker pan.
5. Choose the Cake or Bake Cycle on your bread maker.
6. Close the lid and start the selected cycle. The bread maker will mix the ingredients, then bake the gingerbread loaf.
7. Once the cycle is complete, carefully remove the bread pan from the machine. Let the gingerbread loaf cool in the pan for about 10 minutes before transferring it to a wire rack to cool completely.
8. Slice the gingerbread loaf and enjoy. It can be served plain, with a dusting of powdered sugar, or accompanied by whipped cream or a dollop of lemon curd for extra flavor.

CHAPTER 06: HOLIDAY BREAD

Pandoro

Prep: 20 Min

Serves: 1 Pandoro

Ingredient:

For the Sponge:
- ¼ cup warm milk (60 ml), 80°F (27°C)
- 1 teaspoon sugar (4.2 g)
- 2 teaspoons active dry yeast (6.4 g)
- ½ cup all-purpose flour (64 g)

For the Dough:
- Sponge mixture (from above)
- ⅔ cup sugar (133 g)
- ½ cup warm milk (120 ml), 80°F (27°C)
- 3 large eggs, room temperature
- 1 teaspoon vanilla extract (5 ml)
- Zest of 1 lemon
- ¾ cup unsalted butter (170 g), softened to room temperature
- 3 cups all-purpose flour (381 g)
- 1 teaspoon salt (5 g)

Instruction:

1. In your bread maker pan, combine ¼ cup warm milk, 1 teaspoon sugar, 2 teaspoons yeast, and ½ cup flour. Select a short cycle or simply let the mixture sit until bubbly and frothy, about 30 minutes.
2. Add Dough Ingredients: To the sponge, add ⅔ cup sugar, ½ cup warm milk, eggs, vanilla extract, lemon zest, softened butter, 3 cups flour, and 1 teaspoon salt. Select the Dough Cycle and start the machine.
3. First Rise: Allow the dough to complete the cycle in the bread maker, which will mix, knead, and let the dough rise.
4. Shape and Second Rise: Once the Dough Cycle is complete, gently deflate the dough and transfer it to a greased Pandoro or other mold. Let it rise in a warm place until it's just below the top of the mold, about 1 hour.
5. Preheat your oven to 350°F (175°C).
6. Bake the Pandoro for 35-40 minutes, or until golden brown and a skewer inserted into the center comes out clean. If the top browns too quickly, cover it loosely with aluminum foil.
7. Allow the Pandoro to cool in the mold for about 10 minutes, then gently unmold and let it cool completely on a wire rack.
8. Dust the Pandoro with powdered sugar before serving to mimic the snowy peaks of the Italian Alps.

Dresden Stollen

Prep: 20 Min

Serves: 1 large Stollen

Ingredient:

For the Dough:
- ¾ cup milk (180 ml), warmed to 27°C (80°F)
- ¼ cup unsalted butter, melted (60 ml)
- 2 large eggs, beaten
- ¼ cup sugar (50 g)
- ½ teaspoon salt (2.5 g)
- 3½ cups bread flour (445 g)
- 2 teaspoons active dry yeast (6.4 g)
- Zest of 1 lemon (about 1 tablespoon or 6 g)
- 1 teaspoon vanilla extract (5 ml)
- ½ teaspoon ground cardamom (1 g)
- ½ cup raisins (80 g)
- ¼ cup chopped almonds (30 g)
- ¼ cup candied orange peel (40 g)
- ¼ cup candied lemon peel (40 g)

For the Filling:
- ½ cup marzipan (about 100 g)

➤ Instruction:

1. Place the warm milk, melted butter, beaten eggs, sugar, salt, lemon zest, vanilla extract, and ground cardamom in the bread maker pan. Add the bread flour over the wet ingredients. Make a small indentation in the flour and add the yeast. Select the Dough Cycle and start the machine. Add the raisins, chopped almonds, candied orange peel, and candied lemon peel at the beep for adding ingredients, or towards the end of the kneading cycle.
2. Shape the Stollen: Once the Dough Cycle is complete, remove the dough from the bread maker. On a lightly floured surface, roll the dough into a large oval shape. Flatten the marzipan into a log and place it down the center of the dough. Fold the dough over the marzipan, pressing to seal.
3. Second Rise: Place the shaped Stollen on a baking sheet lined with parchment paper. Cover loosely with a clean kitchen towel and let it rise in a warm place until nearly doubled in size, about 45-60 minutes.
4. Preheat your oven to 175°C (350°F). Bake the Stollen in the preheated oven for 30-40 minutes, or until it is golden brown and sounds hollow when tapped on the bottom.
5. Allow the Stollen to cool on a wire rack. Traditionally, Stollen is dusted with powdered sugar before serving. Slice and enjoy as part of your holiday celebrations.

CHAPTER 06: HOLIDAY BREAD

Simnel Bread

Prep: 15 Min

Serves: 1 loaf

Ingredient:

- 1 cup milk (240 ml), warmed to 80°F (27°C)
- ¼ cup unsalted butter, melted (60 ml)
- 2 large eggs
- ½ cup sugar (100 g)
- ½ teaspoon salt (2.5 g)
- 3½ cups bread flour (445 g)
- 1½ teaspoons active dry yeast (4.65 g)
- 1 teaspoon ground cinnamon (2.6 g)
- ½ teaspoon ground nutmeg (1.2 g)
- 1 cup mixed dried fruit (currants, raisins, and chopped apricots) (160 g)
- Zest of 1 lemon
- Zest of 1 orange

For Marzipan:
- 200 g marzipan, divided into two parts

➤ Instruction:

1. Place the milk, melted butter, eggs, sugar, salt, bread flour, yeast, cinnamon, nutmeg, dried fruits, and citrus zests into the bread maker pan in the order recommended by your manufacturer. Select the Sweet Bread Cycle and start the machine.
2. Shape Marzipan: While the bread is kneading, take half of the marzipan and roll it into a long rope or cylinder that will fit within the length of the bread pan. Set aside.
3. Insert Marzipan: Once the dough cycle completes its final kneading and before the final rise, pause the machine and insert the marzipan rope into the center of the dough, gently pushing it down. Resume the cycle to allow the bread to finish.
4. After the cycle completes, remove the bread from the machine and preheat your oven to 375°F (190°C). Roll out the remaining marzipan into a circle the size of the bread top and place it on the bread. Use a kitchen torch or preheated oven to lightly brown the marzipan, watching carefully to prevent burning.
5. Allow the bread to cool before slicing. Traditionally, Simnel Bread is decorated with 11 marzipan balls representing the true disciples of Jesus, excluding Judas. This can be done before the final browning step.

Kerststol

Prep: 15 Min

Serves: 1 large Stollen

Ingredient:

- 1 cup warm milk (240 ml), 80°F (27°C)
- 2 tablespoons sugar (25 g)
- 2 large eggs, beaten
- 4 tablespoons unsalted butter, melted (60 ml)
- 4 cups bread flour (508 g)
- 2 teaspoons active dry yeast (6.4 g)
- ½ teaspoon salt (2.5 g)
- 1 teaspoon ground cinnamon (2.6 g)
- Zest of 1 lemon
- Zest of 1 orange
- 1 cup mixed dried fruits (raisins, currants, chopped apricots, and cranberries) (160 g)
- ½ cup chopped nuts (almonds or walnuts) (65 g)

Ingredients for Filling:
- 200 g almond paste (or marzipan, if preferred)

For Glazing (Optional):
- 1 egg yolk, beaten for egg wash
- Powdered sugar for dusting

Instruction:

1. Place the warm milk, sugar, beaten eggs, melted butter, bread flour, yeast, salt, cinnamon, lemon zest, and orange zest into the bread maker pan in the order recommended by your manufacturer. Select the Dough Cycle and start the machine. Add the mixed dried fruits and chopped nuts when there's about 5-10 minutes left in the kneading cycle, or at the beep for adding ingredients.
2. Shape the Kerststol: Once the Dough Cycle is complete, remove the dough and roll it out on a lightly floured surface into a large oval shape. Roll the almond paste into a log and place it down the center of the dough. Fold the dough over the almond paste, pressing to seal.
3. Second Rise: Place the shaped dough on a baking sheet lined with parchment paper. Cover with a clean kitchen towel and let it rise in a warm place until nearly doubled in size, about 45-60 minutes.
4. Preheat your oven to 350°F (175°C).
5. Brush the loaf with beaten egg yolk for a glossy finish. Bake in the preheated oven for 30-35 minutes, or until the Kerststol is golden brown and sounds hollow when tapped on the bottom.
6. Allow the Kerststol to cool on a wire rack. Dust with powdered sugar before serving.

CHAPTER 06: HOLIDAY BREAD

Galette des Rois

Prep: 20 Min

Serves: 8

Ingredient:

- 100 g unsalted butter, softened
- 100 g sugar (50 g for conversion accuracy)
- 2 large eggs
- 200 g almond flour
- 2 tablespoons rum (30 ml)
- 1 teaspoon vanilla extract (5 ml)

Additional Ingredients:
- 2 sheets of puff pastry (store-bought or homemade)
- 1 whole almond or bean (to hide inside as the fève)
- 1 beaten egg for egg wash

Instruction:

1. Prepare the Frangipane: In the bread maker pan, combine the softened butter and sugar. Use a Dough or Mix cycle to cream them together. Add the eggs, one at a time, followed by the almond flour, rum, and vanilla extract. Let the bread maker mix until you have a smooth frangipane. If your bread maker has a custom cycle that allows for mixing without heat, use that. Otherwise, mix briefly just to combine ingredients.
2. Preheat your oven to 200°C (390°F).
3. Assemble the Galette: Roll out one sheet of puff pastry and place it on a baking sheet lined with parchment paper. Spread the frangipane evenly over the pastry, leaving a border. Hide the almond or bean somewhere in the frangipane. Cover with the second sheet of puff pastry, pressing the edges to seal. Use a knife to create a decorative pattern on top and brush with beaten egg for a glossy finish.
4. Bake in the preheated oven for 25-30 minutes, or until the pastry is golden and puffed up.
5. Allow the Galette des Rois to cool slightly before serving. Traditionally, the person who finds the almond or bean becomes the king or queen of the day and wears a paper crown.

Almond Flour Bread

Prep: 10 Min

Serves: 1 loaf (12 slices)

Ingredient:

- 1¼ cups warm water (310 ml), 27°C (80°F)
- ¼ cup olive oil (60 ml)
- 3 tablespoons honey (45 ml)
- 3 large eggs, room temperature
- 3 cups almond flour (360 g)
- 1 cup tapioca flour (120 g)
- 1 tablespoon xanthan gum (9 g) (if not included in your gluten-free flour blend)
- 1½ teaspoons salt (7.5 g)
- 2½ teaspoons active dry yeast (7.5 g)

Instruction:

1. In the bread maker pan, add the warm water, olive oil, honey, and eggs. These liquid ingredients will help to bind the dry ingredients and add moisture to the bread.
2. Over the wet ingredients, add the almond flour, tapioca flour, xanthan gum (if using), and salt. It's crucial to distribute these evenly to ensure proper mixing.
3. Make a small well in the center of the dry ingredients (not too deep) and add the yeast to this well, ensuring it doesn't come into direct contact with the liquid ingredients initially.
4. Choose the Gluten-Free Cycle on your bread maker. This cycle is specifically designed for gluten-free bread recipes, providing the necessary kneading, rising, and baking times for a loaf that doesn't contain gluten. Close the lid and start the selected cycle. The machine will mix, knead, rise, and bake the almond flour bread.
5. Once the baking cycle is complete, carefully remove the bread pan from the machine. Let the almond flour bread cool in the pan for about 10 minutes before transferring it to a wire rack to cool completely.
6. Slice the bread and enjoy. Almond Flour Bread is excellent when fresh and can be served with a variety of spreads or used as the base for sandwiches, offering a hearty and nutritious gluten-free option.

CHAPTER 07: GLUTEN-FREE BREAD

Buckwheat Bread

Prep: 10 Min

Serves: 1 loaf (12 slices)

Ingredient:

- 1¼ cups warm water (310 ml), 27°C (80°F)
- 3 tablespoons olive oil (45 ml)
- 3 tablespoons honey (63 g) or sugar (38 g for conversion accuracy)
- 2 large eggs, beaten
- 1 teaspoon salt (5 g)
- 1½ cups buckwheat flour (180 g)
- 1½ cups gluten-free all-purpose flour (180 g)
- 1 teaspoon xanthan gum (if not included in your gluten-free flour blend) (4 g)
- 2½ teaspoons active dry yeast (7.5 g)

Instruction:

1. In the bread maker pan, add the warm water, olive oil, honey (or sugar), and beaten eggs. These liquid ingredients help to moisten the gluten-free flours and add richness to the bread.
2. Add Dry Ingredients: Sprinkle the salt, buckwheat flour, gluten-free all-purpose flour, and xanthan gum over the wet ingredients. Xanthan gum is essential for gluten-free baking as it helps to bind the ingredients and improve the bread's texture.
3. Add Yeast: Make a small well in the center of the dry ingredients (not too deep) and add the yeast to this well, ensuring it doesn't come into direct contact with the liquid ingredients initially.
4. Choose the Gluten-Free Cycle on your bread maker.
5. Close the lid and start the cycle. The machine will mix, knead (gently), rise, and bake the bread.
6. Once the baking cycle is complete, carefully remove the bread pan from the machine. Let the bread cool in the pan for about 10 minutes before transferring it to a wire rack to cool completely.
7. Slice the Buckwheat Bread and enjoy. It's delicious when fresh and can be served with a variety of spreads or used as the base for sandwiches.

Coconut Flour Bread

Prep: 10 Min

Serves: 1 loaf (8-10 slices)

Ingredient:

- 6 large eggs, room temperature
- ½ cup unsalted butter, melted (120 ml)
- 2 tablespoons honey (30 ml) or sugar (25 g for conversion accuracy)
- ¾ cup coconut flour (90 g)
- ¼ cup almond flour (25 g)
- 1 teaspoon baking powder (4 g)
- ½ teaspoon salt (2.5 g)
- 1 cup water (240 ml), 27°C (80°F)

 ## Instruction:

1. In a large bowl, whisk together the eggs, melted butter, and honey (or sugar) until fully combined. The mixture should be uniform and slightly frothy.
2. In a separate bowl, sift together the coconut flour, almond flour, baking powder, and salt to ensure there are no lumps and everything is evenly distributed.
3. Gradually add the dry ingredients to the wet mixture, stirring continuously to prevent clumping. Once combined, add the water and mix until you have a smooth, consistent batter.
4. Pour the batter into the bread maker pan. If your bread maker has a paddle designed for quick breads or cakes, ensure it's in place.
5. Choose the Gluten-Free or Quick Bread Cycle on your bread maker. Close the lid and start the cycle. The machine will mix and bake the bread.
6. Once the baking cycle is complete, carefully remove the bread pan from the machine. Let the coconut flour bread cool in the pan for about 10 minutes before transferring it to a wire rack to cool completely.
7. Slice the bread and enjoy. Coconut flour bread is delicious toasted and can be served with a variety of toppings such as butter, jam, or honey.

CHAPTER 07: GLUTEN-FREE BREAD

Brown Rice Flour Bread

Prep: 10 Min

Serves: 1 loaf (12 slices)

Ingredient:

- 1¼ cups warm water (310 ml), 27°C (80°F)
- ¼ cup olive oil (60 ml)
- 3 tablespoons honey (45 ml)
- 3 large eggs, room temperature
- 2 cups brown rice flour (240 g)
- 1 cup tapioca flour (120 g)
- 1 tablespoon xanthan gum (9 g) (if not included in your gluten-free flour blend)
- 1½ teaspoons salt (7.5 g)
- 2½ teaspoons active dry yeast (7.5 g)

 ## Instruction:

1. In the bread maker pan, add the warm water, olive oil, honey, and eggs. These ingredients will help to bind the dry ingredients and add moisture to the bread.
2. Over the wet ingredients, add the brown rice flour, tapioca flour, xanthan gum (if using), and salt. It's crucial to distribute these evenly to ensure proper mixing.
3. Make a small well in the center of the dry ingredients (not too deep) and add the yeast to this well, ensuring it doesn't come into direct contact with the liquid ingredients initially.
4. Choose the Gluten-Free Cycle on your bread maker.
5. Start the Bread Maker: Close the lid and start the selected cycle. The machine will mix, knead, rise, and bake the brown rice flour bread.
6. Once the baking cycle is complete, carefully remove the bread pan from the machine. Let the bread cool in the pan for about 10 minutes before transferring it to a wire rack to cool completely. This rest period helps the structure of the bread to set, ensuring slices hold together well.
7. Slice the bread and enjoy. Gluten-Free Brown Rice Flour Bread is excellent when fresh and pairs well with a variety of spreads or as the base for sandwiches, offering a hearty and nutritious gluten-free option.

Quinoa Bread

Prep: 10 Min

Serves: 1 loaf (12 slices)

Ingredient:

- 1¼ cups warm water (310 ml), 27°C (80°F)
- ¼ cup olive oil (60 ml)
- 3 tablespoons honey (45 ml)
- 3 large eggs, room temperature
- 2 cups quinoa flour (240 g)
- 1 cup tapioca flour (120 g)
- 1 tablespoon xanthan gum (9 g) (if not included in your gluten-free flour blend)
- 1½ teaspoons salt (7.5 g)
- 2½ teaspoons active dry yeast (7.5 g)

Instruction:

1. Combine Wet Ingredients: In the bread maker pan, add the warm water, olive oil, honey, and eggs. These ingredients will help to bind the flours and add moisture to the bread.
2. Add Dry Ingredients: Over the wet ingredients, add the quinoa flour, tapioca flour, xanthan gum (if using), and salt. It's crucial to distribute these evenly to ensure proper mixing.
3. Add Yeast: Make a small well in the center of the dry ingredients (not too deep) and add the yeast to this well, ensuring it doesn't come into direct contact with the liquid ingredients initially.
4. Select the Gluten-Free Cycle: Choose the Gluten-Free Cycle on your bread maker.
5. Close the lid and start the selected cycle. The machine will mix, knead, rise, and bake the quinoa bread.
6. Cool Before Slicing: Once the baking cycle is complete, carefully remove the bread pan from the machine. Let the quinoa bread cool in the pan for about 10 minutes before transferring it to a wire rack to cool completely.
7. Slice the quinoa bread and enjoy. Gluten-Free Quinoa Bread is excellent when fresh and pairs well with a variety of spreads or as the base for sandwiches, offering a hearty and nutritious gluten-free option.

CHAPTER 07: GLUTEN-FREE BREAD

Teff Bread

Prep: 10 Min

Serves: 1 loaf (12 slices)

Ingredient:

- 1¼ cups warm water (310 ml), 27°C (80°F)
- 2 tablespoons olive oil (30 ml)
- 2 tablespoons honey (30 ml) or maple syrup (40 ml for conversion accuracy)
- 1½ cups teff flour (180 g)
- 1 cup brown rice flour (120 g)
- ½ cup tapioca starch (60 g)
- 1 teaspoon salt (5 g)
- 2½ teaspoons xanthan gum (if not included in your flour blend) (6.25 g)
- 2 teaspoons active dry yeast (6.4 g)
- 3 large eggs, beaten

Instruction:

1. Place the warm water, olive oil, and honey (or maple syrup) into the bread maker pan.
2. Add Dry Ingredients: Over the liquids, add the teff flour, brown rice flour, tapioca starch, salt, and xanthan gum. Make a small well in the center of the dry ingredients and add the yeast.
3. Incorporate Eggs: Gently pour the beaten eggs over the dry ingredients. If your bread maker has a mixing cycle before the baking cycle starts, it will combine these for you. Otherwise, lightly mix the ingredients before starting the cycle.
4. Choose the Gluten-Free Cycle on your bread maker.
5. Start the Bread Maker: Close the lid and start the cycle. The machine will mix, knead, rise, and bake the Teff Bread.
6. Cool Before Slicing: Once the baking cycle is complete, carefully remove the bread pan from the machine. Let the Teff Bread cool in the pan for about 10 minutes before transferring it to a wire rack to cool completely.
7. Serve: Slice the bread and enjoy. Teff Bread has a unique, nutty, and slightly sweet flavor, making it excellent for sandwiches or toasted with a spread of your choice.

Oat Bread

Prep: 10   Min

Serves: 1 loaf (12 slices)

Ingredient:

- 1¼ cups warm water (310 ml), 27°C (80°F)
- 3 tablespoons olive oil (45 ml)
- 2 tablespoons honey (30 ml)
- 3 cups certified gluten-free oat flour (360 g) (If you don't have oat flour, you can make your own by grinding certified gluten-free oats in a food processor until fine.)
- 1 teaspoon salt (5 g)
- 1 tablespoon sugar (12.5 g)
- 2½ teaspoons active dry yeast (7.5 g)
- 3 large eggs, beaten
- 1 teaspoon cider vinegar (5 ml)
- 1½ teaspoons xanthan gum (if not included in your flour blend) (4.5 g)

➤ Instruction:

1. Pour the warm water, olive oil, and honey into the bread maker pan. Then, add the beaten eggs and cider vinegar. These ingredients help to moisten the oat flour and ensure the bread has a tender crumb.
2. Add Dry Ingredients: Over the wet ingredients, add the oat flour, ensuring it's evenly spread. Sprinkle the salt, sugar, and xanthan gum (if using) over the flour. Make a small well in the center of the dry ingredients and add the yeast to this well, ensuring it doesn't touch the liquid directly.
3. Select the Gluten-Free Cycle: Choose the Gluten-Free Cycle on your bread maker.
4. Close the lid and start the selected cycle. The bread maker will take care of the mixing, kneading, rising, and baking processes.
5. Once the baking cycle is complete, carefully remove the bread pan from the machine. Let the oat bread cool in the pan for about 10 minutes before transferring it to a wire rack to cool completely. This rest period helps the structure of the bread to set, ensuring slices hold together well.
6. Slice the oat bread and enjoy it fresh, or toast it for a delicious breakfast. Oat bread pairs wonderfully with both sweet and savory toppings.

CHAPTER 07: GLUTEN-FREE BREAD

Sorghum Bread

Prep: 10   Min

Serves: 1 loaf (12 slices)

Ingredient:

- 1 cup warm water (240 ml), 27°C (80°F)
- 1/4 cup olive oil (60 ml)
- 3 tablespoons honey (45 ml)
- 2 large eggs, room temperature
- 1 teaspoon cider vinegar (5 ml)
- 2 cups sorghum flour (240 g)
- 1 cup tapioca flour (120 g)
- 1/2 cup brown rice flour (80 g)
- 1 tablespoon xanthan gum (if not included in your flour blend) (9 g)
- 1 1/2 teaspoons salt (7.5 g)
- 2 1/4 teaspoons active dry yeast (7 g)

➤ Instruction:

1. Combine Wet Ingredients: In the bread maker pan, add the warm water, olive oil, honey, eggs, and cider vinegar. These liquid ingredients help to moisten the gluten-free flours and contribute to the structure of the bread.
2. Add Dry Ingredients: Over the wet ingredients, carefully add the sorghum flour, tapioca flour, brown rice flour, xanthan gum (if using), and salt. It's important to distribute these evenly to ensure proper mixing.
3. Add Yeast: Make a small well in the center of the dry ingredients (not too deep) and add the yeast to this well, ensuring it doesn't come into direct contact with the liquid ingredients immediately.
4. Select the Gluten-Free Cycle: Choose the Gluten-Free Cycle on your bread maker.
5. Close the lid and start the selected cycle. The machine will mix, knead, rise, and bake the sorghum bread.
6. Once the baking cycle is complete, carefully remove the bread pan from the machine. Let the bread cool in the pan for about 10 minutes before transferring it to a wire rack to cool completely. This helps the bread set and improves its slicing quality.
7. Slice the sorghum bread and enjoy. It's delicious when fresh and can be served with a variety of spreads or used as the base for sandwiches.

Amaranth Bread

Prep: 10 Min

Serves: 1 loaf (12 slices)

Ingredient:

- 1 cup warm water (240 ml), 27°C (80°F)
- 3 tablespoons olive oil (45 ml)
- 2 tablespoons honey (30 ml)
- 3 large eggs, room temperature
- 1 teaspoon cider vinegar (5 ml)
- 1½ cups amaranth flour (180 g)
- 1 cup tapioca flour (120 g)
- ½ cup brown rice flour (80 g)
- 1 tablespoon xanthan gum (9 g) (if not included in your flour blend)
- 1½ teaspoons salt (7.5 g)
- 2½ teaspoons active dry yeast (7.5 g)

Instruction:

1. Combine Wet Ingredients: In the bread maker pan, add the warm water, olive oil, honey, eggs, and cider vinegar. These liquid ingredients will help to bind the gluten-free flours and add moisture to the bread.
2. Add Dry Ingredients: Over the wet ingredients, carefully add the amaranth flour, tapioca flour, brown rice flour, xanthan gum (if using), and salt. It's important to distribute these evenly to ensure proper mixing.
3. Add Yeast: Make a small well in the center of the dry ingredients (not too deep) and add the yeast to this well, ensuring it doesn't come into direct contact with the liquid ingredients immediately.
4. Choose the Gluten-Free Cycle on your bread maker.
5. Close the lid and start the selected cycle. The machine will mix, knead, rise, and bake the amaranth bread.
6. Once the baking cycle is complete, carefully remove the bread pan from the machine. Let the bread cool in the pan for about 10 minutes before transferring it to a wire rack to cool completely. This helps the bread set and improves its slicing quality.
7. Slice the amaranth bread and enjoy. It's delicious when fresh and pairs well with both sweet and savory toppings.

CHAPTER 07: GLUTEN-FREE BREAD

Chickpea Flour Bread

Prep: 10 Min

Serves: 1 loaf (12 slices)

Ingredient:

- 1¼ cups water (310 ml), warmed to 27°C (80°F)
- 3 tablespoons olive oil (45 ml)
- 2 tablespoons honey (30 ml)
- 3 large eggs
- 2 cups chickpea flour (also known as garbanzo bean flour) (240 g)
- 1 cup tapioca flour (120 g)
- 1 tablespoon xanthan gum (if not included in your flour blend) (9 g)
- 1½ teaspoons salt (7.5 g)
- 2½ teaspoons active dry yeast (7.5 g)

Instruction:

1. Combine Wet Ingredients: In the bread maker pan, add the warmed water, olive oil, honey, and eggs. These ingredients help to moisten the chickpea flour and ensure the bread has a tender crumb.
2. Add Dry Ingredients: Over the wet ingredients, add the chickpea flour, tapioca flour, xanthan gum (if using), and salt. It's important to distribute these evenly to ensure proper mixing.
3. Add Yeast: Make a small well in the center of the dry ingredients (not too deep) and add the yeast to this well, ensuring it doesn't come into direct contact with the liquid ingredients initially.
4. Choose the Gluten-Free Cycle on your bread maker.
5. Close the lid and start the cycle. The machine will mix, knead, rise, and bake the chickpea flour bread.
6. Once the baking cycle is complete, carefully remove the bread pan from the machine. Let the chickpea flour bread cool in the pan for about 10 minutes before transferring it to a wire rack to cool completely. This rest period helps the structure of the bread to set, ensuring slices hold together well.
7. Slice the bread and enjoy. Chickpea flour bread is delicious when fresh and can be served with a variety of spreads or used as the base for sandwiches.

Millet Bread

Prep: 10 Min

Serves: 1 loaf (12 slices)

Ingredient:

- 1 cup warm water (240 ml), 27°C (80°F)
- 2 tablespoons olive oil (30 ml)
- 3 tablespoons honey (45 ml)
- 2 large eggs, beaten
- 1½ cups millet flour (180 g)
- 1 cup tapioca flour (120 g)
- ½ cup brown rice flour (80 g)
- 1 teaspoon salt (5 g)
- 2½ teaspoons xanthan gum (7.5 g) (if your flour blend doesn't include it)
- 2½ teaspoons active dry yeast (7.5 g)

▶ Instruction:

1. Combine Wet Ingredients: In the bread maker pan, add the warm water, olive oil, honey, and beaten eggs. These ingredients help to moisten the gluten-free flours and ensure the bread has a tender crumb.
2. Add Dry Ingredients: Over the wet ingredients, add the millet flour, tapioca flour, brown rice flour, salt, and xanthan gum (if using). It's important to distribute these evenly to ensure proper mixing.
3. Add Yeast: Make a small well in the center of the dry ingredients (not too deep) and add the yeast to this well, ensuring it doesn't come into direct contact with the liquid ingredients immediately.
4. Choose the Gluten-Free Cycle on your bread maker.
5. Close the lid and start the selected cycle. The machine will mix, knead, rise, and bake the millet bread.
6. Once the baking cycle is complete, carefully remove the bread pan from the machine. Let the millet bread cool in the pan for about 10 minutes before transferring it to a wire rack to cool completely. This rest period helps the structure of the bread to set, ensuring slices hold together well.
7. Slice the bread and enjoy. Millet bread pairs well with both sweet and savory toppings and can be served as part of any meal.

CHAPTER 07: GLUTEN-FREE BREAD

Paleo Bread

Prep: 10 Min

Serves: 1 loaf (12 slices)

Ingredient:

- 1 cup warm water (240 ml), 27°C (80°F)
- 5 large eggs
- 2 tablespoons olive oil (30 ml)
- 2 tablespoons honey (30 ml) (optional, some Paleo diets may exclude honey)
- 1 teaspoon apple cider vinegar (5 ml)
- 2 cups almond flour (200 g)
- ⅔ cup coconut flour (80 g)
- ¼ cup ground flaxseed meal (30 g)
- 1 teaspoon baking soda (5 g)
- ½ teaspoon salt (2.5 g)

▶ Instruction:

1. Prepare the Liquid Mixture: In a large bowl, whisk together the warm water, eggs, olive oil, honey (if using), and apple cider vinegar until well combined.
2. Combine Dry Ingredients: In a separate bowl, mix the almond flour, coconut flour, ground flaxseed meal, baking soda, and salt.
3. Add Wet Ingredients to Bread Maker: Pour the liquid mixture into the bread maker pan.
4. Add Dry Ingredients: Gently spoon the dry ingredients on top of the liquid mixture in the bread maker pan.
5. Mix Before Baking: If your bread maker has a mixing feature, use it to combine the ingredients before baking. If not, you might want to mix the ingredients in a separate bowl and then transfer the batter to the bread maker pan to ensure even mixing.
6. Choose the Gluten-Free or Quick Bread cycle on your bread maker. Close the lid and start the selected cycle. The machine will bake the Paleo bread.
7. Once the baking cycle is complete, carefully remove the bread pan from the machine. Let the Paleo bread cool in the pan for about 10 minutes before transferring it to a wire rack to cool completely.
8. Slice the bread and enjoy. This Paleo bread is great for sandwiches or toasted with a spread of almond butter or avocado.

Multi-Seed Bread

Prep: 10 Min

Serves: 1 loaf (12 slices)

Ingredient:

- 1¼ cups warm water (310 ml), 27°C (80°F)
- 3 tablespoons olive oil (45 ml)
- 2 tablespoons honey (30 ml)
- 2 large eggs, room temperature
- 2 cups gluten-free all-purpose flour (240 g)
- 1 cup brown rice flour (120 g)
- 1 tablespoon xanthan gum (if not included in your gluten-free flour blend) (9 g)
- 1½ teaspoons salt (7.5 g)
- 1 tablespoon active dry yeast (9.45 g)
- ¼ cup flaxseeds (40 g)
- ¼ cup sunflower seeds (35 g)
- 2 tablespoons pumpkin seeds (18 g)
- 2 tablespoons sesame seeds (18 g)
- 2 tablespoons poppy seeds (18 g)

Instruction:

1. Combine Wet Ingredients: In the bread maker pan, add the warm water, olive oil, honey, and eggs. These liquid ingredients help to bind the gluten-free flours and add moisture to the bread.
2. Add Dry Ingredients: Over the wet ingredients, add the gluten-free all-purpose flour, brown rice flour, xanthan gum (if using), and salt. It's crucial to distribute these evenly to ensure proper mixing.
3. Incorporate Seeds: Add the flaxseeds, sunflower seeds, pumpkin seeds, sesame seeds, and poppy seeds to the mixture. These will be mixed into the dough during the kneading cycle.
4. Add Yeast: Make a small well in the center of the dry ingredients (not too deep) and add the yeast to this well, ensuring it doesn't come into direct contact with the liquid ingredients immediately.
5. Choose the Gluten-Free Cycle on your bread maker.
6. Close the lid and start the selected cycle. The machine will mix, knead, rise, and bake the Multi-Seed Bread.
7. Once the baking cycle is complete, carefully remove the bread pan from the machine. Let the bread cool in the pan for about 10 minutes before transferring it to a wire rack to cool completely. This rest period helps the structure of the bread to set, ensuring slices hold together well.
8. Slice the Multi-Seed Bread and enjoy.

CHAPTER 07: GLUTEN-FREE BREAD

Cassava Flour Bread

Prep: 10 Min

Serves: 1 loaf (12 slices)

Ingredient:

- 1¼ cups warm water (310 ml), 27°C (80°F)
- ¼ cup olive oil (60 ml)
- 2 tablespoons honey (30 ml)
- 3 large eggs, room temperature
- 3 cups cassava flour (360 g)
- 1 tablespoon xanthan gum (9 g) (if your gluten-free flour blend doesn't include it)
- 1½ teaspoons salt (7.5 g)
- 2½ teaspoons active dry yeast (7.5 g)

Instruction:

1. Combine Wet Ingredients: In the bread maker pan, add the warm water, olive oil, honey, and eggs. These ingredients help to moisten the cassava flour and ensure the bread is tender.
2. Add Dry Ingredients: Over the wet ingredients, add the cassava flour, xanthan gum (if using), and salt. It's crucial to distribute these evenly to ensure proper mixing.
3. Add Yeast: Make a small well in the center of the dry ingredients (not too deep) and add the yeast to this well, ensuring it doesn't come into direct contact with the liquid ingredients initially.
4. Select the Gluten-Free Cycle: Choose the Gluten-Free Cycle on your bread maker.
5. Start the Bread Maker: Close the lid and start the selected cycle. The machine will mix, knead, rise, and bake the cassava flour bread.
6. Cool Before Slicing: Once the baking cycle is complete, carefully remove the bread pan from the machine. Let the cassava flour bread cool in the pan for about 10 minutes before transferring it to a wire rack to cool completely. This rest period helps the structure of the bread to set, ensuring slices hold together well.
7. Slice the cassava flour bread and enjoy. This loaf is excellent when fresh and pairs well with both sweet and savory toppings.

Flaxseed Bread

Prep: 10   Min

Serves: 1 loaf (12 slices)

Ingredient:

- 1¼ cups warm water (310 ml), 27°C (80°F)
- ¼ cup olive oil (60 ml)
- 3 tablespoons honey (45 ml)
- 3 large eggs
- 1 cup ground flaxseeds (150 g)
- 2 cups gluten-free all-purpose flour (240 g)
- ½ cup almond flour (50 g)
- 1 tablespoon xanthan gum (if not included in your gluten-free flour blend) (9 g)
- 1½ teaspoons salt (7.5 g)
- 2½ teaspoons active dry yeast (7.5 g)

➤ Instruction:

1. Pour the warm water, olive oil, and honey into the bread maker pan. Add the eggs, ensuring they're lightly beaten before adding.
2. Add Dry Ingredients: Over the wet mixture, carefully add the ground flaxseeds, gluten-free all-purpose flour, almond flour, xanthan gum (if using), and salt. It's essential to distribute these evenly to ensure proper mixing.
3. Add Yeast: Make a small well in the center of the dry ingredients (not too deep) and add the yeast to this well, ensuring it doesn't come into direct contact with the liquid ingredients initially.
4. Select the Gluten-Free Cycle: Choose the Gluten-Free Cycle on your bread maker. Close the lid and start the selected cycle. The machine will mix, knead, rise, and bake the flaxseed bread.
5. Once the baking cycle is complete, carefully remove the bread pan from the machine. Let the flaxseed bread cool in the pan for about 10 minutes before transferring it to a wire rack to cool completely. This rest period helps the structure of the bread to set, ensuring slices hold together well.
6. Slice the bread and enjoy. Gluten-Free Flaxseed Bread is delicious when fresh and can be served with a variety of spreads or used as the base for sandwiches.

CHAPTER 07: GLUTEN-FREE BREAD

Hemp Bread

Prep: 10   Min

Serves: 1 loaf (12 slices)

Ingredient:

- 1¼ cups warm water (310 ml), 27°C (80°F)
- ¼ cup olive oil (60 ml)
- 2 tablespoons honey (30 ml)
- 3 large eggs, room temperature
- 1½ cups gluten-free all-purpose flour (180 g)
- 1 cup brown rice flour (120 g)
- ½ cup hemp hearts (hulled hemp seeds) (80 g)
- 1 tablespoon xanthan gum (if not included in your gluten-free flour blend) (9 g)
- 1½ teaspoons salt (7.5 g)
- 2½ teaspoons active dry yeast (7.5 g)

➤ Instruction:

1. Combine Wet Ingredients: In the bread maker pan, add the warm water, olive oil, honey, and eggs. These liquid ingredients will help to bind the gluten-free flours and add moisture to the bread.
2. Add Dry Ingredients: Over the wet ingredients, add the gluten-free all-purpose flour, brown rice flour, hemp hearts, xanthan gum (if using), and salt. It's crucial to distribute these evenly to ensure proper mixing.
3. Add Yeast: Make a small well in the center of the dry ingredients (not too deep) and add the yeast to this well, ensuring it doesn't come into direct contact with the liquid ingredients initially.
4. Choose the Gluten-Free Cycle on your bread maker.
5. Close the lid and start the selected cycle. The machine will mix, knead, rise, and bake the hemp bread.
6. Once the baking cycle is complete, carefully remove the bread pan from the machine. Let the hemp bread cool in the pan for about 10 minutes before transferring it to a wire rack to cool completely. This rest period helps the structure of the bread to set, ensuring slices hold together well.
7. Slice the hemp bread and enjoy. This bread is excellent when fresh and pairs well with both sweet and savory toppings.

Potato Bread

Prep: 15 Min

Serves: 1 loaf (12 slices)

Ingredient:

- 1 cup warm water (240 ml), 27°C (80°F)
- ½ cup mashed potatoes (prepared from boiled potatoes and cooled) (120 ml)
- ¼ cup olive oil (60 ml)
- 2 tablespoons honey (30 ml)
- 2 large eggs, room temperature
- 1½ cups gluten-free all-purpose flour (180 g)
- 1 cup tapioca flour (120 g)
- ½ cup potato starch (not flour) (80 g)
- 1 tablespoon xanthan gum (if not included in your gluten-free flour blend) (9 g)
- 1½ teaspoons salt (7.5 g)
- 2½ teaspoons active dry yeast (7.5 g)

Instruction:

1. Boil potatoes until tender, mash them without any added liquid or butter, and allow to cool. Measure ½ cup for the recipe.
2. Combine Wet Ingredients: In the bread maker pan, add the warm water, mashed potatoes, olive oil, honey, and eggs. These ingredients add moisture and richness to the bread.
3. Add Dry Ingredients: Over the wet ingredients, add the gluten-free all-purpose flour, tapioca flour, potato starch, xanthan gum (if using), and salt. Distribute these evenly to ensure proper mixing.
4. Add Yeast: Make a small well in the center of the dry ingredients (not too deep) and add the yeast to this well, ensuring it doesn't come into direct contact with the liquid ingredients initially.
5. Choose the Gluten-Free Cycle on your bread maker.
6. Close the lid and start the selected cycle. The machine will mix, knead, rise, and bake the potato bread.
7. Once the baking cycle is complete, carefully remove the bread pan from the machine. Let the potato bread cool in the pan for about 10 minutes before transferring it to a wire rack to cool completely. This rest period helps the structure of the bread to set, ensuring slices hold together well.
8. Slice the potato bread and enjoy.

CHAPTER 07: GLUTEN-FREE BREAD

Rice Bran Bread

Prep: 10 Min

Serves: 1 loaf (12 slices)

Ingredient:

- 1 cup warm water (240 ml), 27°C (80°F)
- ¼ cup olive oil (60 ml)
- 3 tablespoons honey (45 ml)
- 3 large eggs, room temperature
- 1 cup rice bran (110 g)
- 2 cups gluten-free all-purpose flour (240 g)
- 1 tablespoon xanthan gum (9 g) (if not included in your gluten-free flour blend)
- 1½ teaspoons salt (7.5 g)
- 2½ teaspoons active dry yeast (7.5 g)

Instruction:

1. In the bread maker pan, add the warm water, olive oil, honey, and eggs. These ingredients help to moisten the flours and add richness to the bread.
2. Add Dry Ingredients: Over the wet ingredients, add the rice bran, gluten-free all-purpose flour, xanthan gum (if using), and salt. It's crucial to distribute these evenly to ensure proper mixing.
3. Add Yeast: Make a small well in the center of the dry ingredients (not too deep) and add the yeast to this well, ensuring it doesn't come into direct contact with the liquid ingredients initially.
4. Choose the Gluten-Free Cycle on your bread maker. This cycle is specifically designed for gluten-free bread recipes, providing the necessary kneading, rising, and baking times for a loaf that doesn't contain gluten.
5. Close the lid and start the selected cycle. The machine will mix, knead, rise, and bake the rice bran bread.
6. Once the baking cycle is complete, carefully remove the bread pan from the machine. Let the rice bran bread cool in the pan for about 10 minutes before transferring it to a wire rack to cool completely. This rest period helps the structure of the bread to set, ensuring slices hold together well.
7. Slice the rice bran bread and enjoy. This loaf is excellent when fresh and pairs well with both sweet and savory toppings, offering a nutritious addition to any meal.

Tapioca Bread

Prep: 10 Min

Serves: 1 loaf (12 slices)

Ingredient:

- 1½ cups warm water (360 ml), 27°C (80°F)
- ¼ cup olive oil (60 ml)
- 3 tablespoons honey (45 ml)
- 2 large eggs, room temperature
- 2½ cups tapioca flour (300 g)
- 1 cup rice flour (120 g)
- 1 tablespoon xanthan gum (if not included in your flour blend) (9 g)
- 1½ teaspoons salt (7.5 g)
- 2½ teaspoons active dry yeast (7.5 g)

Instruction:

1. Combine Wet Ingredients: In the bread maker pan, add the warm water, olive oil, honey, and eggs. These liquid ingredients help to moisten the flours and add richness to the bread.
2. Add Dry Ingredients: Over the wet ingredients, add the tapioca flour, rice flour, xanthan gum (if using), and salt. It's crucial to distribute these evenly to ensure proper mixing.
3. Add Yeast: Make a small well in the center of the dry ingredients (not too deep) and add the yeast to this well, ensuring it doesn't come into direct contact with the liquid ingredients initially.
4. Choose the Gluten-Free Cycle on your bread maker. This cycle is designed for gluten-free bread recipes, accommodating their unique mixing, kneading, and rising requirements.
5. Close the lid and start the selected cycle. The machine will mix, knead, rise, and bake the tapioca bread.
6. Once the baking cycle is complete, carefully remove the bread pan from the machine. Let the tapioca bread cool in the pan for about 10 minutes before transferring it to a wire rack to cool completely. This rest period helps the structure of the bread to set, ensuring slices hold together well.
7. Slice the tapioca bread and enjoy.

CHAPTER 07: GLUTEN-FREE BREAD

Pumpernickel Gluten-Free Bread

Prep: 10 Min

Serves: 1 loaf (12 slices)

Ingredient:

- 1¼ cups warm water (310 ml), 27°C (80°F)
- 2 tablespoons molasses (30 ml) for color and sweetness
- 3 tablespoons olive oil (45 ml)
- 2 large eggs, room temperature
- 1 cup buckwheat flour (120 g)
- 1 cup gluten-free all-purpose flour (120 g)
- ½ cup almond flour (50 g)
- ¼ cup cocoa powder (for color) (22 g)
- 1 tablespoon ground flaxseed (7 g) for texture
- 1 teaspoon salt (5 g)
- 2 teaspoons instant espresso powder (optional, for depth of flavor) (4 g)
- 1 tablespoon caraway seeds (optional, for authentic flavor) (9 g)
- 1 tablespoon xanthan gum (if not included in your flour blend) (9 g)
- 2½ teaspoons active dry yeast (7.5 g)

Instruction:

1. In the bread maker pan, add the warm water, molasses, olive oil, and eggs. These ingredients help to moisten the gluten-free flours and add to the richness of the bread.
2. Over the wet ingredients, add the buckwheat flour, gluten-free all-purpose flour, almond flour, cocoa powder, ground flaxseed, salt, espresso powder (if using), caraway seeds (if using), and xanthan gum (if using). It's important to distribute these evenly to ensure proper mixing.
3. Make a small well in the center of the dry ingredients (not too deep) and add the yeast to this well, ensuring it doesn't come into direct contact with the liquid ingredients initially.
4. Choose the Gluten-Free Cycle on your bread maker. Close the lid and start the selected cycle.
5. Once the baking cycle is complete, carefully remove the bread pan from the machine. Let the bread cool in the pan for about 10 minutes before transferring it to a wire rack to cool completely. This rest period helps the structure of the bread to set, ensuring slices hold together well.
6. Slice the pumpernickel-style gluten-free bread and enjoy. This loaf is excellent when fresh and pairs well with both sweet and savory toppings, offering the distinctive pumpernickel flavor in a gluten-free format.

Sunflower Seed Bread

Prep: 10 Min

Serves: 1 loaf (12 slices)

Ingredient:

- 1¼ cups warm water (310 ml), 27°C (80°F)
- 3 tablespoons olive oil (45 ml)
- 2 tablespoons honey (30 ml)
- 3 large eggs, room temperature
- 2 cups gluten-free all-purpose flour (240 g)
- 1 cup almond flour (100 g)
- ½ cup ground flaxseeds (60 g) for added fiber and nutrition
- 1 tablespoon xanthan gum (9 g) (if not included in your gluten-free flour blend)
- 1½ teaspoons salt (7.5 g)
- 2½ teaspoons active dry yeast (7.5 g)
- ¾ cup raw sunflower seeds (105 g), plus extra for topping.

Instruction:

1. In the bread maker pan, add the warm water, olive oil, honey, and eggs. These ingredients will help to bind the flours and add moisture to the bread.
2. Over the wet ingredients, carefully add the gluten-free all-purpose flour, almond flour, ground flaxseeds, xanthan gum (if using), and salt. Distribute these evenly to ensure proper mixing.
3. Make a small well in the center of the dry ingredients (not too deep) and add the yeast to this well, ensuring it doesn't come into direct contact with the liquid ingredients immediately. Then, sprinkle the sunflower seeds into the mixture, reserving some for topping the bread before baking.
4. Select the Gluten-Free Cycle. Close the lid and start the selected cycle. If your bread maker has an option to add ingredients (like nuts or seeds) later in the cycle, add the reserved sunflower seeds at this prompt. Otherwise, they can be mixed in with the rest of the ingredients from the start.
5. Once the baking cycle is complete, carefully remove the bread pan from the machine. Let the sunflower seed bread cool in the pan for about 10 minutes before transferring it to a wire rack to cool completely. This rest period helps the structure of the bread to set, ensuring slices hold together well.
6. Slice the bread and enjoy. Sunflower Seed Bread is delicious when fresh and pairs well with both sweet and savory toppings.

CHAPTER 07: GLUTEN-FREE BREAD

Psyllium Husk Bread

Prep: 10 Min

Serves: 1 loaf (12 slices)

Ingredient:

- 1¼ cups warm water (310 ml), 27°C (80°F)
- ¼ cup olive oil (60 ml)
- 2 tablespoons honey (30 ml)
- 3 large eggs, room temperature
- 2 cups gluten-free all-purpose flour (240 g)
- ½ cup almond flour (50 g)
- ¼ cup psyllium husk powder (28 g)
- 1 tablespoon xanthan gum (9 g) (if not included in your gluten-free flour blend)
- 1½ teaspoons salt (7.5 g)
- 2½ teaspoons active dry yeast (7.5 g)

Instruction:

1. In the bread maker pan, add the warm water, olive oil, honey, and eggs. These liquid ingredients will help to bind the dry ingredients and add moisture to the bread.
2. Add Dry Ingredients: Over the wet ingredients, add the gluten-free all-purpose flour, almond flour, psyllium husk powder, xanthan gum (if using), and salt. It's crucial to distribute these evenly to ensure proper mixing.
3. Add Yeast: Make a small well in the center of the dry ingredients (not too deep) and add the yeast to this well, ensuring it doesn't come into direct contact with the liquid ingredients initially.
4. Select the Gluten-Free Cycle. Close the lid and start the selected cycle. The machine will mix, knead, rise, and bake the psyllium husk bread.
5. Once the baking cycle is complete, carefully remove the bread pan from the machine. Let the psyllium husk bread cool in the pan for about 10 minutes before transferring it to a wire rack to cool completely. This rest period helps the structure of the bread to set, ensuring slices hold together well.
6. Slice the bread and enjoy. Psyllium Husk Bread is excellent when fresh and can be served with a variety of spreads or used as the base for sandwiches.

Nut Bread (e.g., walnut, pecan)

Prep: 10 Min

Serves: 1 loaf (12 slices)

Ingredient:

- 1¼ cups warm water (310 ml), 27°C (80°F)
- ¼ cup olive oil (60 ml)
- 3 tablespoons honey (45 ml)
- 3 large eggs, room temperature
- 2 cups gluten-free all-purpose flour (240 g)
- 1 cup almond flour (100 g) - for added nuttiness and moisture
- 1 tablespoon xanthan gum (9 g) (if not included in your gluten-free flour blend)
- 1½ teaspoons salt (7.5 g)
- 2½ teaspoons active dry yeast (7.5 g)
- 1 cup mixed nuts (walnuts and pecans), roughly chopped (150 g)

Instruction:

1. Roughly chop the walnuts and pecans, or your choice of nuts, and set aside.
2. Combine Wet Ingredients: In the bread maker pan, add the warm water, olive oil, honey, and eggs. These ingredients help to bind the gluten-free flours and add moisture to the bread.
3. Add Dry Ingredients: Over the wet ingredients, add the gluten-free all-purpose flour, almond flour, xanthan gum (if using), and salt. It's crucial to distribute these evenly to ensure proper mixing.
4. Add Yeast: Make a small well in the center of the dry ingredients (not too deep) and add the yeast to this well, ensuring it doesn't come into direct contact with the liquid ingredients initially.
5. Add Nuts: Sprinkle the chopped nuts over the top. If your bread maker has a nut dispenser, use it to add the nuts at the correct time during the kneading process. Otherwise, they can be added from the start.
6. Select the Gluten-Free Cycle. Close the lid and start the selected cycle. The machine will mix, knead, rise, and bake the nut bread.
7. Once the baking cycle is complete, carefully remove the bread pan from the machine. Let the nut bread cool in the pan for about 10 minutes before transferring it to a wire rack to cool completely.
8. Serve: Slice the nut bread and enjoy. This loaf is excellent when fresh and pairs well with both sweet and savory toppings, making it a versatile addition to any meal.

CHAPTER 07: GLUTEN-FREE BREAD

Chia Seed Bread

Prep: 10 Min

Serves: 1 loaf (12 slices)

Ingredient:

- 1¼ cups warm water (310 ml), 27°C (80°F)
- ¼ cup olive oil (60 ml)
- 2 tablespoons honey (30 ml)
- 3 large eggs, room temperature
- 2 cups gluten-free all-purpose flour (240 g)
- ½ cup ground chia seeds (80 g)
- ½ cup almond flour (50 g)
- 1 tablespoon xanthan gum (9 g) (if not included in your gluten-free flour blend)
- 1½ teaspoons salt (7.5 g)
- 2½ teaspoons active dry yeast (7.5 g)

Instruction:

1. Combine Wet Ingredients: In the bread maker pan, add the warm water, olive oil, honey, and eggs. These ingredients will help to moisten the flours and ensure a tender crumb in the final bread.
2. Add Dry Ingredients: Over the wet ingredients, add the gluten-free all-purpose flour, ground chia seeds, almond flour, xanthan gum (if using), and salt. Distribute these evenly to ensure proper mixing.
3. Add Yeast: Make a small well in the center of the dry ingredients (not too deep) and add the yeast to this well, ensuring it doesn't come into direct contact with the liquid ingredients initially.
4. Select the Gluten-Free Cycle: Choose the Gluten-Free Cycle on your bread maker.
5. Close the lid and start the selected cycle. The machine will mix, knead, rise, and bake the chia seed bread.
6. Once the baking cycle is complete, carefully remove the bread pan from the machine. Let the chia seed bread cool in the pan for about 10 minutes before transferring it to a wire rack to cool completely. This rest period helps the structure of the bread to set, ensuring slices hold together well.
7. Slice the bread and enjoy. Gluten-Free Chia Seed Bread is excellent when fresh and pairs well with both sweet and savory toppings.

Lentil Bread

Prep: 15   Min

Serves: 1 loaf (12 slices)

Ingredient:

- 1¼ cups warm water (310 ml), 27°C (80°F)
- ¼ cup olive oil (60 ml)
- 2 tablespoons honey (30 ml)
- 3 large eggs, room temperature
- 1½ cups lentil flour (made from ground dry lentils) (180 g)
- 1 cup gluten-free all-purpose flour (120 g)
- ½ cup tapioca flour (60 g)
- 1 tablespoon xanthan gum (if not included in your gluten-free flour blend) (9 g)
- 1½ teaspoons salt (7.5 g)
- 2½ teaspoons active dry yeast (7.5 g)

➤ Instruction:

1. If you're making lentil flour at home, grind the dry lentils until they reach a fine, powdery consistency. Measure out 1½ cups for the recipe.
2. Combine Wet Ingredients: In the bread maker pan, add the warm water, olive oil, honey, and eggs. These ingredients help to moisten the flours and add richness to the bread.
3. Add Dry Ingredients: Over the wet ingredients, carefully add the lentil flour, gluten-free all-purpose flour, tapioca flour, xanthan gum (if using), and salt. It's essential to distribute these evenly to ensure proper mixing.
4. Add Yeast: Make a small well in the center of the dry ingredients (not too deep) and add the yeast to this well, ensuring it doesn't come into direct contact with the liquid ingredients initially.
5. Select the Gluten-Free Cycle. Close the lid and start the selected cycle. The machine will mix, knead, rise, and bake the lentil bread.
6. Once the baking cycle is complete, carefully remove the bread pan from the machine. Let the lentil bread cool in the pan for about 10 minutes before transferring it to a wire rack to cool completely.
7. Slice the bread and enjoy. Gluten-Free Lentil Bread is excellent when fresh and can be served with a variety of spreads or used as the base for sandwiches, offering a hearty and nutritious alternative to traditional bread.

CHAPTER 07: GLUTEN-FREE BREAD

Zucchini Bread

Prep: 15   Min

Serves: 1 loaf (8–10 slices)

Ingredient:

- 1½ cups grated zucchini (from about 1 medium zucchini) (360 ml after draining)
- 3 large eggs, room temperature
- ¼ cup olive oil (60 ml)
- ¼ cup unsweetened applesauce (60 ml) - for added moisture and natural sweetness
- ¾ cup sugar (150 g) - adjust based on preference
- 2 teaspoons vanilla extract (10 ml)
- 2 cups gluten-free all-purpose flour (240 g)
- 1 teaspoon xanthan gum (4.5 g) (if not included in your gluten-free flour blend)
- 1½ teaspoons baking powder (7.5 g)
- ½ teaspoon baking soda (2.5 g)
- 1 teaspoon ground cinnamon (2.6 g)
- ¼ teaspoon ground nutmeg (0.5 g)
- ½ teaspoon salt (2.5 g)

➤ Instruction:

1. Grate the zucchini and let it sit in a colander to drain any excess moisture. Squeeze gently to remove moisture before measuring.
2. Combine Wet Ingredients: In a mixing bowl, whisk together the eggs, olive oil, applesauce, sugar, and vanilla extract. Pour this mixture into the bread maker pan.
3. Add Dry Ingredients: Over the wet ingredients, gently add the gluten-free all-purpose flour, xanthan gum (if using), baking powder, baking soda, cinnamon, nutmeg, and salt. Ensure even distribution of ingredients for consistent mixing.
4. Add Zucchini: Last, evenly distribute the grated zucchini over the top of the dry ingredients.
5. Select the Cake or Quick Bread Cycle. Close the lid and start the selected cycle. The bread maker will mix the ingredients and then bake the zucchini bread.
6. Once the cycle is complete, carefully remove the bread pan from the machine. Let the zucchini bread cool in the pan for about 10 minutes before transferring it to a wire rack to cool completely. This helps the bread set and improves slicing.
7. Slice the zucchini bread and enjoy. This loaf is delicious on its own or served with a spread of butter or cream cheese

Pumpkin Bread

Prep: 10   Min

Serves: 1 loaf (8-10 slices)

Ingredient:

- 1 cup pumpkin puree (240 ml)
- 3 large eggs, room temperature
- ¼ cup vegetable oil (60 ml)
- ¼ cup unsweetened applesauce (60 ml) - for added moisture
- ¾ cup sugar (150 g) - adjust according to taste
- 1 teaspoon vanilla extract (5 ml)
- 2 cups gluten-free all-purpose flour (240 g)
- 1 teaspoon xanthan gum (4.5 g) (if not included in your gluten-free flour blend)
- 1½ teaspoons baking powder (7.5 g)
- ½ teaspoon baking soda (2.5 g)
- 2 teaspoons ground cinnamon (5.2 g)
- ¼ teaspoon ground nutmeg (0.5 g)
- ¼ teaspoon ground ginger (0.5 g)
- ¼ teaspoon ground cloves (0.5 g)
- ½ teaspoon salt (2.5 g)

Instruction:

1. In a mixing bowl, whisk together the pumpkin puree, eggs, vegetable oil, applesauce, sugar, and vanilla extract. Pour this mixture into the bread maker pan.
2. Add Dry Ingredients: Over the wet ingredients, gently add the gluten-free all-purpose flour, xanthan gum (if using), baking powder, baking soda, cinnamon, nutmeg, ginger, cloves, and salt. Ensure even distribution of ingredients for consistent mixing.
3. Select the Cake or Quick Bread Cycle: Choose the Cake or Quick Bread cycle on your bread maker. This cycle is designed for non-yeast bread, allowing for mixing and baking without a rise time.
4. Start the Bread Maker: Close the lid and start the selected cycle. The bread maker will mix the ingredients and then bake the pumpkin bread.
5. Cool Before Slicing: Once the cycle is complete, carefully remove the bread pan from the machine. Let the pumpkin bread cool in the pan for about 10 minutes before transferring it to a wire rack to cool completely. This helps the bread set and improves slicing.
6. Serve: Slice the pumpkin bread and enjoy. This loaf is delightful when served warm, with a spread of butter or cream cheese, making it a perfect treat for breakfast or a snack.

CHAPTER 07: GLUTEN-FREE BREAD

Olive Bread

Prep: 15   Min

Serves: 1 loaf (12 slices)

Ingredient:

- 1¼ cups warm water (310 ml), 27°C (80°F)
- 3 tablespoons olive oil (45 ml), plus extra for drizzling
- 2 tablespoons honey (30 ml) or sugar (25 g for conversion accuracy)
- 3 large eggs, room temperature
- 2 cups gluten-free all-purpose flour (240 g)
- 1 cup almond flour (100 g)
- 1 tablespoon xanthan gum (9 g) (if not included in your gluten-free flour blend)
- 1½ teaspoons salt (7.5 g)
- 2½ teaspoons active dry yeast (7.5 g)
- 1 cup chopped olives (green, black, or a mix) (150 g), drained and patted dry

Instruction:

1. Chop the olives and pat them dry with paper towels to remove excess moisture. This prevents the bread from becoming too soggy.
2. In the bread maker pan, add the warm water, olive oil, honey (or sugar), and eggs. These ingredients help to bind the gluten-free flours and add moisture to the bread.
3. Over the wet ingredients, add the gluten-free all-purpose flour, almond flour, xanthan gum (if using), and salt. It's crucial to distribute these evenly to ensure proper mixing.
4. Make a small well in the center of the dry ingredients (not too deep) and add the yeast to this well, ensuring it doesn't come into direct contact with the liquid ingredients initially.
5. Sprinkle the chopped olives over the top. If your bread maker has a mix-in feature, use it to add the olives at the correct time during the kneading process. Otherwise, they can be added from the start.
6. Select the Gluten-Free Cycle. Close the lid and start the selected cycle. The machine will mix, knead, rise, and bake the olive bread.
7. Once the baking cycle is complete, carefully remove the bread pan from the machine. Let the olive bread cool in the pan for about 10 minutes before transferring it to a wire rack to cool completely. Slice the olive bread and enjoy.

Cinnamon Raisin Bread

Prep: 10 Min

Serves: 1 loaf (12 slices)

Ingredient:

- 1 cup warm milk (240 ml), 27°C (80°F)
- 3 large eggs, room temperature
- ¼ cup unsalted butter, melted (60 ml)
- ¼ cup honey (60 ml)
- 2 teaspoons vanilla extract (10 ml)
- 3 cups gluten-free all-purpose flour (360 g)
- 1 tablespoon xanthan gum (9 g) (if not included in your gluten-free flour blend)
- 2 teaspoons ground cinnamon (5.2 g)
- 1½ teaspoons salt (7.5 g)
- 2½ teaspoons active dry yeast (7.5 g)
- 1 cup raisins (150 g)

Instruction:

1. In a bowl, whisk together the warm milk, eggs, melted butter, honey, and vanilla extract. Pour this mixture into the bread maker pan.
2. Add the Dry Ingredients: Over the liquid mixture, gently add the gluten-free all-purpose flour, xanthan gum (if using), ground cinnamon, and salt. Ensure even distribution of ingredients for consistent mixing.
3. Add the Yeast: Make a small well in the center of the dry ingredients (not too deep) and add the yeast to this well, ensuring it doesn't come into direct contact with the liquid ingredients initially.
4. Add Raisins: If your bread maker has a fruit and nut dispenser, add the raisins there. If not, wait until the bread maker signals to add mix-ins, usually towards the end of the kneading cycle, to add them directly into the pan.
5. Select the Gluten-Free Cycle. Close the lid and start the selected cycle. The machine will mix, knead, rise, and bake the cinnamon raisin bread.
6. Once the baking cycle is complete, carefully remove the bread pan from the machine. Let the cinnamon raisin bread cool in the pan for about 10 minutes before transferring it to a wire rack to cool completely.
7. Slice the cinnamon raisin bread and enjoy. This loaf is delicious when served warm, with a spread of butter or cream cheese.

CHAPTER 07: GLUTEN-FREE BREAD

Cornbread (gluten-free version)

Prep: 10 Min

Serves: 1 loaf (8–10 slices)

Ingredient:

- 1 cup milk (240 ml), warmed to 27°C (80°F)
- ¼ cup unsalted butter, melted (60 ml)
- 2 large eggs, room temperature
- 1 cup gluten-free cornmeal (120 g)
- 1 cup gluten-free all-purpose flour (120 g)
- ½ cup sugar (100 g)
- 2 teaspoons baking powder (10 g)
- ½ teaspoon salt (2.5 g)
- ¼ cup honey (60 ml) - optional for added sweetness

Instruction:

1. In a medium bowl, whisk together the milk, melted butter, and eggs. If using, stir in the honey into this liquid mixture for added sweetness.
2. Combine Dry Ingredients: In another bowl, mix the gluten-free cornmeal, gluten-free all-purpose flour, sugar, baking powder, and salt. Ensure they are well combined to distribute the leavening agent evenly.
3. Add to Bread Maker: Pour the liquid ingredients into the bread maker pan first, followed by the dry ingredients on top. This order helps prevent the dry ingredients from sticking to the bottom of the pan.
4. Choose the Cake or Quick Bread cycle on your bread maker. This cycle is designed for non-yeast bread, allowing for mixing and baking without a rise time.
5. Close the lid and start the selected cycle. The bread maker will mix the ingredients and then bake the cornbread.
6. Once the cycle is complete, carefully remove the bread pan from the machine. Let the cornbread cool in the pan for about 10 minutes before transferring it to a wire rack to cool completely. Cooling helps the bread set and improves its slicing quality.
7. Slice the cornbread and enjoy. This gluten-free cornbread is perfect when served warm, with a spread of butter or alongside your favorite dishes.

Made in the USA
Middletown, DE
06 January 2025

68969886R00046